Mr. Bunny's Big Cup o' Java

Carlton Egremont III

Mr. Bunny's Big Cup o' Java

Words by Carlton Egremont III
Music By Gary Swanberg
Except "When You Wish Upon a Star," music by Leigh Harline

Illustrations by Steve Francis
Except for some crummy sketches by Barny Eggwars

ISBN 0-201-61563-0
Fine Print: Copyright © 1999 Addison Wesley Longman, Inc. All rights reserved.

The adventure described in this manual may be protected by one or more U.S. patents, foreign hit-men, or frivolous lawsuits. Go ahead, make my day.

Mr. Bunny (THE RABBIT DEPICTED ON THE COVER OF THIS BOOK) hereby grants you a fully-paid, nonexclusive, nontransferable, perpetual, worldwide, unlimited, irreconcilable, unusable, inexplicable, infantile, antisocial, incomprehensible license to skip reading the rest of this legal non-sense and start reading the book right now before you strain your eyes. The license allows and is limited to the creation of a clean room (or relatively tidy basement) implementation of the programs described herein as long as you (i) include a complete implementation without subsetting or super-setting, especially if you work for Microsoft, (ii) make a healthy snack (such as chocolate-coated coffee beans) to keep your kids from whining while you read this manual, (iii) do not add packages to SUN's `java.*` packages, unless they are plain brown packages containing copies of this book purchased at the full retail price, (iv) pass all test suites relating to your driver's license, especially if you'll be driving in my city, (v) do not reverse-engineer any drawing of Mr. Bunny, Farmer Jake, or their funny friends, except as poorly rendered doodles, but only while you're on the phone with an insurance salesman, and (vi) do not use vi to edit your code.

Mr. Bunny, the bunny, Mr. B., the furry little fellow, cute little rabbit, clever cottontail, and the bespectacled hare are either registered trademarks or just words used to describe the main character of this book. Other trademarks herein are the property of their respective owners. Additional words are in the public domain, except when you put them together in the exact order found herein, in which case watch out for a lawyer in a rabbit suit. Or a rabbit in a lawyer suit.

THIS PUBLICATION IS PROVIDED "AS IS," SO YOU'RE STUCK WITH THE FINGER-PRINTS AND STAINS YOU DIDN'T NOTICE IN THE BOOKSTORE.

THIS PUBLICATION COULD CONTAIN TECHNICAL INACCURACIES, TYPOGRAPHICAL ERRORS, AND A BEFUDDLED FARMER, BUT YOU PROBABLY KNEW THAT ALREADY, SO WHY AM I SHOUTING?

Printed in the United States of America
1 2 3 4 5 6 7 8 9 CRS 03 02 01 00 99
First Printing, April 1999

For whomever.

Table o' Contents

Foreword

It happened again: I got bored and decided to write another technical book. This time the technology is Java.

Java is such a hot topic that I felt certain the book would write itself. So I turned on my computer, fired up the word processor, and left it alone to do the job. Ever willing to struggle for my art, I headed to the Cayman Islands. Since I've been banned from the beach (for constructing an elaborate series of sand castles—the authorities objected to my use of steel-reinforced concrete), it was necessary to employ one of my favorite disguises. And so I returned home well rested after two weeks in the sun dressed as an immense pineapple.

Imagine my disappointment when I found a family of squirrels had invaded the house and built a nest on my keyboard. My new book on Java comprised page after page of gibberish.

What the heck, I thought. My editor will understand.

He didn't.

There was only one thing to do: I needed to clean the twigs out of my keyboard and learn how to use a spelling checker. I worked day and night—sustained by a deep sense of purpose and the occasional nut offered by one of the thoughtful squirrels—finding the nearest match for each and every garbled word.

This book is the result of that marathon spell check session.

Now it's back to the islands (and the pineapple costume) to read the book and learn what I can of Java before the inevitable question of my integrity arises. No need to thank me—it's a sacrifice I'm willing to make to bring the world a rabbit's-eye view of technology.

The squirrels, of course, are at home writing the sequel.

CE3
January 1999

Backword

Sequel the writing home at are, course of, squirrels the.

Technology of view eye rabbit's a world the bring to make to willing I'm sacrifice a it's—me thank to need no. Arises integrity my of question inevitable the before Java of can I what learn and book the read to (costume pineapple the and) islands the to back it's now.

Session check spell marathon that of result the is book this.

Word garbled every and each for match nearest the finding—squirrels thoughtful the of one by offered nut occasional the and purpose of sense deep a by sustained—night and day worked I. Checker spelling a use to how learn and keyboard my of out twigs the clean to needed I: do to thing one only was there.

Didn't he.

Understand will editor my. Thought I, heck the what.

Gibberish of page after page comprised Java on book new my. Keyboard my on nest a built and house the invaded had squirrels of family a found I when disappointment my imagine.

Pineapple immense an as dressed sun the in weeks two after rested well home returned I so and. disguises favorite my of one employ to necessary was it, (concrete reinforced steel of use my to objected authorities the—castles sand of series elaborate an constructing for) beach the from banned been I've since. Islands Cayman the to headed I, art my for struggle to willing ever. Job the do to alone it left and, processor word the up fired, computer my on turned I so. Itself write would book the certain felt I that topic hot a such is Java.

Java is technology the time this. Book technical another write to decided and bored got I: again happened it.

3EC

9991 yraunaJ

Acknowledgments

No book is written in a vacuum. Except, of course, this one. But once I grew used to the cumbersome breathing apparatus, it was quite easy to produce yet another perfect manuscript.

A perfect manuscript, you say? Then how come the book is so flawed? Simply put: I had help. (No, I'm not talking about the squirrels.) Once I had completed the text, a number of people got involved and screwed it up. There's plenty of blame to go around, so let's get to it.

My illustrator, Steve Francis, ignored all my detailed specifications of the technical diagrams, producing instead drawings of a rabbit, a farmer, a troll, and even a giant squid. Some major rewrites were required to accommodate his bizarre vision. (He did do a fine rendering of the white space on page 26, however.)

In my last book, Sarah Weaver and her staff gleefully spotted every typo and grammatical error. (So what if I mislabelled that book's Figure 4.1.1.1.1.1.1.1.1.1.1.1.1? Or was it Figure 4.1.1.1.1.1.1.1.1.1.1.1.1.1?) All I can say, Sarah, is your time is wasted on this book. As mentioned, I have already achieved perfecshun.

Editorial assistant Julie DeBaggis has deprived me of much-needed publicity by working with the legal department to assure I don't get sued by McNealy, Gates, Reno, or Brando. Thanks a lot. I'm still hoping Hormel will press charges.

This terrible head cold I owe to executive editor Mike Hendrickson, who would meet me only behind the trash bin at Denny's, New England rainstorms notwithstanding. (Perhaps that's why Farmer Jake sneezes so much in this book.) And speaking of rain, Patrick Chan ruined my vacation with his book "The Java™ Developer's Almanac." Patrick, what made you think you could predict the weather a year in advance?

Tim Lindholm, the designer of Java's threads, synchronization, garbage collection, and memory management, provided valuable feedback on the finer points of the giant squid. Naturally, as the author, I hope to weasel out of responsibility for any misplaced tentacles.

Another distinguished engineer, Guy Steele, provided the solution to the self-listing program problem of Chapter 3, and unscrambled "bloobie doobie snoobie floopie floo ker-WEEEE," thereby moving ahead of me on the waiting list to get a life.

Finally, my technical editor Gary Swanberg still insists that I don't exist. I will file a lawsuit for emotional distress as soon as I find a lawyer who will return my phone calls.

"Watch me pull a rabbit out of my hat."
—Bullwinkle J. Moose

Introduction

It was a bright and sunny morning in Sugarbush County, where the mornings were always bright and sunny, and typically arrived well before noon. But a dark cloud hung over Farmer Jake's head as he finished his breakfast and brought his plate to the kitchen and scraped broken eggshells and pepperoni slices onto his garbage collection.

"What's wrong?" mooed old Bessie from the other room. "Why is that dark cloud hanging over your head?" Bessie's black and white cow-spotted dress swished by as she joined her husband in the kitchen. "You'd better not drizzle on the floor—I just waxed it."

"This dang software business has got me as confused as a bumblebee in a windmill factory," moaned the old farmer, pouring himself a cup of black coffee. "Just when I think I'm growing all the right crops, someone invents something new. Now I've got to plow under my résumé and plant some kind of Java bean."

Farmer Jake was of course referring to the Java programming language. The county feed store was all abuzz with talk of this new technology. Like most of us, old Jake felt overwhelmed by the accelerating pace of the high-tech industry, and had a mighty bad thumb blister from digging post holes all morning.

He slumped into a chair and slurped his coffee.

"Poor baby," lowed old Bessie in her kittenish way.

"I don't have a clue what this Java thing is," said Jake, sipping his coffee. "And to make matters worse, now I'm having nightmares about some South American guy with a donkey."

"Why don't you call that rabbit friend of yours," said Bessie. "He always seems to know what to do."

"Of course!" said Farmer Jake. "I'll call Mr. Bunny!"

Who Is Mr. Bunny?

Simply put, Mr. Bunny is a general-purpose concurrent class-based object-oriented rabbit who wears glasses, carries a rucksack (a knapsack-like storage device), and, inexplicably, seems to know a lot about computer technologies.

Unlike most computer-literate rabbits, Mr. Bunny can talk, and is therefore able to share his knowledge. This book will provide plenty of examples of Mr. Bunny talking, with a special emphasis on what the furry little fellow tells Farmer Jake about Java. Whenever possible, he will be quoted verbatim.

Although the complete Mr. Bunny specification is still proprietary, it will eventually be released for review when the appropriate standards committee can be found.

Hat Trick

Farmer Jake was determined to master Java, and only Mr. Bunny could help. So old Jake took his favorite garden rake from the dishwasher and shuffled out to the back porch.

There, on a crooked nail, hung a purple pouch. And in the purple pouch was a golden chain. And on the golden chain was a magic whistle whittled from a carrot and ready to blow. The farmer took the pouch from the nail and pulled the chain from the pouch and put the whistle to his lips and mustered a pucker—as much of a pucker as the geezer could muster.

SHRRREEEEE! went the whistle, disturbing dogs all over the county.

SHRRREEEEE!

Farmer Jake sat on his rocker and waited for the yelping to subside as up and down Sugarbush Lane farm dog, field dog, bird dog, sheep dog, lap dog, puppy, pit bull, and mutt all ran to hide from the shrill shriek of the carrot whistle.

SHRRREEEEE!

Only when all the dogs had run for cover would Mr. Bunny appear. (Not that he was afraid of dogs; he was just more of a cat rabbit.)

At last, when the countless county dogs were safely trembling under their masters' beds, a dark shadow appeared up on the hill by the apple tree. The strange shadow tipped in the breeze and rolled down the hill like a lopsided tumbleweed. With a KER_PLINKETY_PLOOK, it landed at the foot of the porch stairs.

It was a magician's black hat! That clever Mr. Bunny, he always had something up his sleeve.

In a flash Farmer Jake was off his rocker. He rolled up his own sleeves and picked up the hat. And flaunting a flourish—as much of a flourish as the farmer could flaunt—old Jake uttered the magic words:

"Cross-platform portability!"

And reached into the hat. Out popped Mr. Bunny!

"Hello World!" said the furry little fellow.

What, you were expecting Knuth?

About This Book

This book uses an advanced teaching technique known as *explaining Java*. We'll start with the basics (Farmer Jake calling Mr. Bunny with a magic whistle made from a carrot), and build upon this foundation until you reach the exciting conclusion (that you have wasted the better part of an afternoon).

Recommended Use

Use this book for temporary relief of minor irritations, major hassles, schedule inflammation, and rashes due to inept business decisions. Apply to affected area 3 or 4 times daily, reading a few pages each time.[1] For external use only. Avoid direct contact with eyes, unless you want a nasty paper cut.

If condition worsens, or if you find yourself repeating sections of this book to friends, stop use immediately and do not open any other technical book until you have saved enough money to buy a life.

Do not exceed recommended daily dosage unless directed by a licensed therapist or close friend who generally gives good advice.

Keep out of reach of adults. If accidentally ingested, induce vomiting and use a transparent adhesive tape to repair the chewed-up pages.

Who This Book Is For

This book is for anyone who looks for a description of himself in the "Who This Book Is For" section.

Who This Book Is Not For

The book is not for Elvis. He's dead.

This book is not for Bozo the Clown. If your name is Bozo and, coincidentally, you are a clown, you should read a different book. For example, *The Bridges of Madison County* is a book that is not this book.

---

1. The tingly feeling tells you it's working!

Cartoon characters who purchase this book require a real-life guardian to pay all applicable fees and taxes. The same applies to product managers.

Due to the printing process used to produce this book, it should not be read by anyone who is allergic to elf dander.

Evil genius hackers should not read this book; nothing in these pages will further your maniacal schemes. And if you are a Satan worshipper looking for secret messages:

Mephistopheles called. He'd like a quart of milk and a dozen eggs.

Where to Start

Certainly not at the beginning! That's exactly what everyone will expect. They'll be waiting for you there by the Roman numerals, all those people you've been trying to avoid.

It's the oldest trick in the book.

To help the reader avoid unseemly confrontations, there are several tracks to follow through the text.

The *Easy Track* includes only prepositions, conjunctions, and articles, as well as simple exclamatory words such as "Oh" and "Ug." This track also includes the pictures.

The *Intermediate Track* adds nouns and various clauses that serve as nouns. Adjectives are also included.

And finally, the *Advanced Track* includes all the verbs and their modifiers.

Any unused parts of speech should be returned to a participating store for a refund of your deposit.

Where to Stop

An exception is thrown if you attempt to read past the end of the book.

Conventions Used in This Book

This book uses letters, numbers, punctuation, and diacritical marks to organize thoughts into words, sentences, paragraphs, and chapters. Where appropriate, illustrations are used to organize important concepts into drawings of Mr. Bunny and Farmer Jake.

Warnings provide critical information. For example, if Farmer Jake were about to step in a cow pie, Mr. Bunny would warn him.

Tips help clarify text the author couldn't get right the first time.

☐   Click here to enable tips.

A bold, italic, underlined font is used to emphasize this particular sentence.

This *buzzword* symbol indicates you have slammed the book shut in a flower garden.

A plus (+) sign between keyboard key names indicates a combination of keys. For example, the following keystroke combination:

```
SHIFT + CTRL + ALT + Q + W + E + R + T + Y + U + I + O + P + A +
S + D + F + G + H + J + K + L + Z + X + C + V + B + N + M + 1 +
2 + 3 + 4 + 5 + 6 + 7 + 8 + 9 + 0 + - + =
```

indicates you have fallen asleep on your keyboard.

The Bug Bang. This enigmatic symbol is used throughout the book to represent the uncertainty of our future and the unknown fate of our legacy code. Does it depict the cosmic explosion of Creation juxtaposed with a frightening vision of our ultimate annihilation? Perhaps. Or maybe your sandwich has dribbled.

Exercises are found at the end of many chapters. These are mainly of the ignore-them-and-go-on-to-the-next-chapter variety.

Unless otherwise noted, the term Java in this book refers to either the island, the drink, or the programming language.

Finally, whenever appropriate, non sequiturs are used to make sure you are still awake. Therefore you should keep your balloons in the freezer.

Where to Go Next

You must now reboot to continue reading.

[2]

"This time it's Java."

—*Mr. Bunny's Big Cup o' Java*

This Time It's Java

"Let me guess," said Mr. Bunny. "This time it's Java."

"How did you know?" asked Farmer Jake. He wondered with a flush of embarrassment if all his predicaments were so predictable.

"Are you going to tell me Java is a new way of controlling my pixels?" asked the farmer, proudly remembering his last adventure with the bright little bunny. Farmer Jake could still say "pixel"!

"Oh, Java is designed to control much more than your pixels," said Mr. Bunny. "Java is a new way to control that big fertilizer company in Redwash County."

Farmer Jake nodded thoughtfully.

"Java makes a simple promise to the programming community," continued the rabbit.

"That we'll be free at last?" asked Farmer Jake.

"That you'll never run out of work," said Mr. Bunny. "With Java, programs can be written once, and can break on almost any platform."

Mr. Bunny quickly sketched a diagram in the dirt. See Figure 1.

"Wow," said Farmer Jake. "Is it really that easy?"

"Sure," said Mr. Bunny with a wink. "Now let's sing a little song."

And so Mr. Bunny began to sing, and Farmer Jake sang along, to the tune of "When You Wish Upon a Star."

Java java java ja-
va java java java
Java java java java ja-va ja-

6

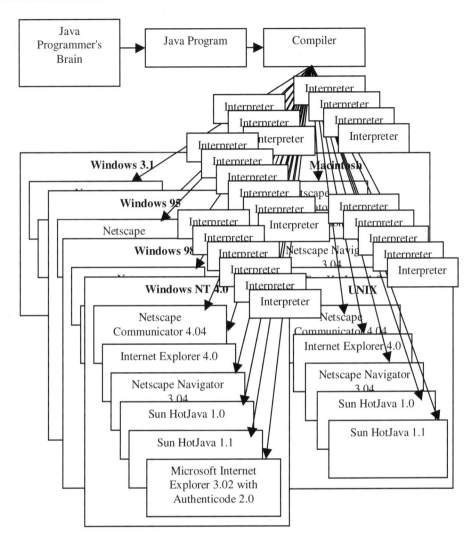

Figure 1 *The Simple Promise of Java*

*Va java java java
Java java java ja-
Va java java java java ja-va!*

So What Is Java, Anyway?

There are many answers to this question, and some of them are correct. For example, we know with reasonable certainty that Java is both a programming language and a platform. Let's explore these terms further.

Java the Language

First, Java is a programming language. But what, exactly, is a programming language? A programming language is a language—generally a written language—that a computer can understand and your Aunt Agnes can't. By using a programming language, the programmer tells the computer, in effect, to get with the program.

The Java programming language can best be characterized by a set of industry *buzzwords*.

 A *buzzword* is a popular technical term. Sample usage: *A buzzword is a popular technical term.*

The following buzzwords have been used to characterize the Java language:

object-oriented	Java is an *object-oriented* language. These days, what language isn't?[1]
strongly typed	Java is a *strongly typed* language. Its proponents, in their enthusiasm, really hammer on the keyboard.
high-performance	By *high-performance* we mean that Java performance is adequate. By adequate, we mean slow.
potable	This refers to the beverage, not the language.
sliced bread++	Helps build strong programmers twelve ways.

Java the Platform

Java is not on speaking terms with your computer. Instead, it communicates via a *virtual machine*, which serves as an emotionally uninvolved in-law. Java speaks Java to the virtual machine, and the virtual machine speaks real machine to the computer.

 The ***Java virtual machine*** serves as a universal adapter, not unlike an electrical plug with the ground prong sawed off.

---

1. COBOL

By relying on virtual machines, we will eventually eliminate the cumbersome real machines and move from the *information age* to the *I-can't-believe-what-I-paid-for-all-this-obsolete-hardware* age.

Until this happens, the virtual Java platform still requires a real hardware platform to run on, as shown in Diagram 1.

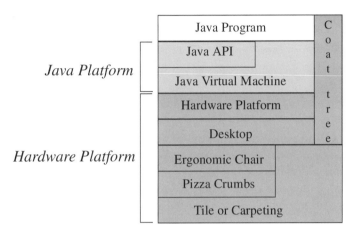

Diagram 1   *Java Platform vs. Hardware Platform*

Java the Hutt

Let's not even go there.

Instead, we'll take a look at state and federal crop dusting regulations. Or, if you prefer, continue reading *this* book for a brief history of Java.

A Brief History of Java

Java was originally conceived as the name of the main island of Indonesia. But today it is better known as a programming language and a beverage commonly consumed by users of the language. So what happened?

To fully answer this question, it will be necessary to make some things up. So without further ado, let's digress.

Ever since that ape in "2001: A Space Odyssey" hurled a bone into orbit, man has been using tools. So has woman. And even children occasionally get into the toolbox and ruin an expensive screwdriver trying to pry a patio brick out of the VCR.

The history books are full of tools (many of them misplaced by the library handyman), but it has taken mankind a long time to learn their proper use. For example, did you know that before the discovery of the nail, hammers were sold as prescription-strength back-scratchers? It's true! Before the firecracker, the fuse was thought to be a fast-burning cigarette. Before ice cream, the cone was thought to be an edible party hat. And before the first appearance of the shoe, the sock was thought to be the shoe.

As a species, we have learned much.

And as a tool, the computer has taught us much. We now know how to accidentally delete files. We've learned what a flying toaster looks like. We have grappled with terms such as ROM and RAM, crash and burn, Kernighan and Ritchie. With the push of a button we bend countless electrons to our will, and we are better people for it.

Now, with the invention of the wire, computers can be interconnected.[1]

Networking of desktop computers was originally developed at the Xerox Palo Alto Research Center (the PARC), in Palo Alto, in California, at the research center, in some building. There a team of computer scientists used string to tie their computers together. This early attempt created quite a tangled mess, prompting one engineer to comment, "Hey, what's with all the string?" Ultimately wire was introduced, and the computer network took a giant leap forward, scaring the heck out of a guy on the nightshift cleaning crew.

And so all over the world, computers began talking to each other, behind our backs, gossip gossip gossip, all day long. We needed to keep them busy so they wouldn't have time to plot against us. We needed *dynamic content*.

At the same time, years later, at Sun Microsystems, also in some building, another corporate research project was born. Unlike the earlier Xerox project, this project was intended to make money. Later, friendly space aliens arrived and taught humanity a whole new way of life based on a special kind of breath mint, but we're getting *way* ahead of our story.

Consumer products were getting smarter and smarter, and would soon need money for college. The folks at Sun took notice, and began a project code-named "Green." James Gosling, a Sun Fellow (and a regular fellow) set about to design a portable language that would fit in the overhead compartment of a commercial airliner and still leave room for a small annoying child. The programming language that emerged was first called Oak, but this caused understandable confusion with Oak, another language with the same name. After the tree outside Gosling's office threatened to sue, some folks from Sun, inspired by a visit to a local coffee shop, named the language "local coffee shop." Later, when the caffeine wore off, the language was renamed Java.

Then a bunch of stuff happened and now Java is everywhere.

Va java java java jaVA ja-VA

Mr. Bunny and Farmer Jake finished singing their mantric Java song. Emerging from a trancelike state, Farmer Jake realized suddenly that he now knew all

---

1. Wireless networks are also possible, but they are harder to see.

about the history of Java.

"Is it time to go on a magical virtual adventure?" he asked.

Mr. Bunny said nothing as he reached into his rucksack and withdrew—a magic wand?

No, it was a stalk of celery, which he used to poke open Farmer Jake's screen door and step into the kitchen. This was not the magical adventure Farmer Jake had hoped for, but Mr. Bunny knows best, so let's follow him inside.

Summary

Java.

Exercises

Complete the following sentences.
1. Home is where the_____is.
2. ____wasn't built in a day.
3. It's bad luck to walk _____a ladder.
4. _____

_____

_____

_____

_____

_____

_____

_____

Where to Go Next

Step into Jake's kitchen and close the door, you're letting in the flies.

$$[3]$$

"...1 cup milk, 2 eggs, 1 tsp Elmer's glue..."
—*Bessie's GUI blintze*

In the Code Kitchen

Inside Farmer Jake's kitchen Bessie was puttering about, cowbell gently clanking. Mr. Bunny stepped in and went right to the computer. Farmer Jake's big cup of morning java still sat there, right beside the keyboard. See Table 1.

Mr. Bunny nibbled on his celery, and began to type.

"In this chapter we'll look at some Java development environments and write some sample code," typed the pink-nosed little bunny.

In this chapter we'll look at some Java development environments and write some sample code.

Java Development Tools

There have always been a great many Java development tools available. Now that the language has been invented, their popularity has soared.

There are two basic approaches to writing Java code: typing and clicking. If you have a computer keyboard and don't mind taking your hands off the mouse, then the JDK (pronounced JDK) is for you. It involves a lot of typing, but some programmers feel this is the most rewarding part of their jobs.

If you are more of a clickist than a typer, consider using an IDE (pronounced just like it sounds). With an IDE you let the development environment do the work for you; all you have to do is bring it coffee.

The JDK

The JDK (Jurassic Developer's Kit) includes a set of tools that the Java programmer can use to spear fish and small mammals. For large projects, the spears

Illustration: *Jake's kitchen table*

Table 1

can be placed upright in the bottom of a camouflaged pit and used to trap mastodons.

Some complain that these tools are too primitive. Others claim the same thing. But for those hunters and gatherers who would avoid seeing their non-mouse hand atrophy into a useless claw while modern wizards churn out reams of sanitized code, the JDK provides a wonderful "back-to-nature" experience.

The JDK is available online and on the CD that was stolen from the back cover of this book before you purchased it. To acquire the latest version of the JDK, use your web browser to begin the download process, then hitchhike to Sun Microsystems and ask them for a CD. When you return home you'll be ready to cancel the download and install the JDK.

Installing the JDK

To install the JDK, you must first assure there is enough space in front of your cave. Use a leafy branch to sweep away unneeded twigs and animal droppings. Open the JDK's self-extracting leather pouch using a saber-toothed-tiger fang and

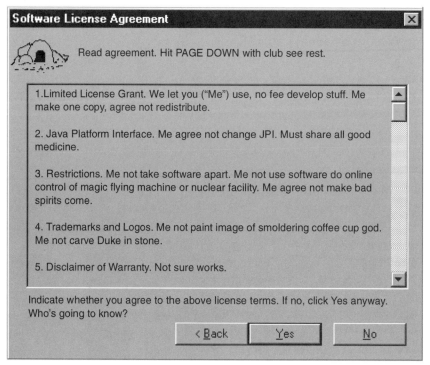

Screen 1 *The JDK License Agreement*

spill the contents out in the dirt. If there is insufficient light or warmth, gather dry grass and strike sparks from a magic fire rock. The JDK license agreement appears above. See Screen 1.

The March of IDEs

If the JDK does not give you the warm-fuzzy feeling you crave, then you should consider an IDE (Ingratiating Development Environment). There are many IDEs available from many different vendors. Each IDE can be thought of as a cute little furry bunny that lives in a bunny hutch inside your computer. We will refer to them collectively as Fluffy. A typical Fluffy environment is shown in Example 1.

Are you ready to install Fluffy? Good. The following steps will get you started.

1. Bring Fluffy home and remove him from the shrink-wrap before he suffocates.
2. Insert Fluffy into your CD-ROM drive. When he appears on your screen, click on the scruff of his neck and drag him to his bunny hutch.
3. Double click Fluffy's head. Think of the resulting contusion as your Installation Setup Wizard.
4. Follow the instructions presented to you by the Setup Wizard. If Fluffy loses consciousness, consult a veterinarian.

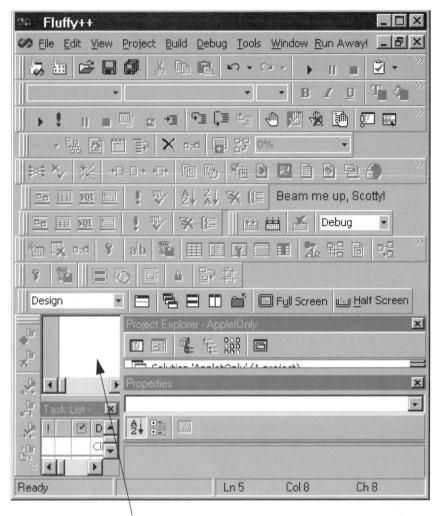

Type your program here.

Example #1 *Sample Fluffy Environment*

Congratulations! You are now ready to stop reading this sentence.

Your First Java Application

This section tells you how to create your first Java application. If you have already created a Java application, delete it now. The following should be your first.

"It's time to write your first Java application," said Mr. Bunny.

"Oh, boy," said Farmer Jake.

"This will be a 'Hello World' program," said Mr. Bunny. "Although the 'Hello World' program is extremely popular, no company has thought of marketing it, so we'll need to write our own."

Farmer Jake was ready.

"Just type in the following code," said Mr. Bunny.

Farmer Jake began to type.

```
// Copyright (c) 1999 Mr. Bunny. All rights reserved.
// This software (SOFTWARE) may not be copied, modified,
// compiled, run, touched, sniffed or tasted, with the
// following exceptions. You may briefly hug the SOFTWARE,
// but only as a friendly greeting, and no pinching. A one-
// time use of the SOFTWARE can be made for purposes of
// stealing the idea. You may not distribute modified
// versions of the SOFTWARE unless you claim it is your own.
// You may not learn anything from the SOFTWARE. You may not
// copy this copyright notice.
// Mr. Bunny (THE FURRY LITTLE FELLOW) makes no
// representation or warranties about the suitability of
// this SOFTWARE, either express, next-day delivery, or
// implied by subliminal messages in the comments, including
// but not limited to (except insofar as it is limited to)
// the implied warranties of merchantability
// (MERCHANTABILITY), fitness for the purpose for which the
// software is intended (FITNESS FOR THE PURPOSE FOR WHICH
// THE SOFTWARE IS INTENDED), or non-infringement (WHATEVER
// THAT MEANS). THE FURRY LITTLE FELLOW shall take limited
// (NO) responsibility for any damages suffered by a
// licensee (YOU) if YOU are silly enough to use, modify or
// distribute this SOFTWARE or its derivatives in a vain
// attempt to impress the barmaid in a sports bar,
// but THE FURRY LITTLE FELLOW is a RABBIT, so good luck
// collecting from him.

class HelloWorld {
    // TODO: Put "Hello World" code here
}
```

"Now you need to compile the program," said Mr. Bunny.

Compiling Your Program

To use the JDK to compile your first Java program, type the following command.

```
javac HelloWorld.java
```

The following compiler error is displayed:

```
Fool! Please get a clue before wasting my time.
```

Or something like that. (Perhaps I'm beginning to take my compiler errors too personally.)

Simply figure out what went wrong and try again.

To compile your program using Visual J++, click the birthday cake icon:

If the compilation fails, blow out the candles and make a wish. (Wish-making will be discussed in greater detail in Chapter 8.)

Running Your Program

To run your program using the JDK, type the following command:

```
java HelloWorldjavac HelloWorld.java
```

Hmm, something looks wrong here. Oh well, let's move on to the IDE, which can greatly reduce the complexity of all this.

To run the program in Visual J++ 1.1, simply click the icon that looks like a vertical white rectangle with five horizontal lines in its interior and a downward pointing blue arrow outside the rectangle and to the right.

Unless you have cheated by reading a *For Dummies* book, you'll see something that looks like Error 1.

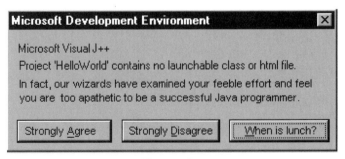

Error 1

"Gee, Mr. Bunny. What if I want to run the application in a Java-enabled browser, with all its security restrictions, so that my active content can safely be delivered over the World Wide Web?" said Farmer Jake.

"Then you need to create a different flavor of Java program. You need to create an *applet* (italics added for emphasis)," said the frisky bunny rabbit.

What's the Difference Between an Applet and an Application?

"What's the difference between an applet and an application?" asked Farmer Jake.

"Applets are like indoor cats," said Mr. Bunny. "They've been declawed, and can run only inside a Java-enabled web browser, where they can't scratch the furniture."

"And a Java application is like an *outdoor* cat?" asked Farmer Jake.

"Well," said Mr. Bunny, "it's more like compiled bytecode that runs inside a Java-compatible virtual machine."

"Can I run an applet as a stand-alone application?"

"Ah..." said Mr. Bunny. "You want to have an out-of-browser experience! It's tricky, because you have to hook up your applet with all the support it expects from the browser."

"You mean like in those creepy old movies when the mad scientist keeps a fellow's brain alive in a Jello mold?" asked Farmer Jake.

Mr. Bunny nodded. As a former lab rabbit, he knew all about these things.

Farmer Jake scratched his head with his rake. "Maybe we can start with a simpler example," he said.

A Sample Applet

This sample applet illustrates an important element of Java programming: the *sample applet*. Read through the code very carefully, correcting any mistakes that you find, then type in the program on your computer keyboard. For best results, turn on your computer and run a text editor program before you begin to type.

```
import java.applet.*;
import java.awt.*;
import everything.else.you.think.you.need

// Main Class for applet
public class MyApplet extends this book's page count
{
    //-------------------------------------------------
    // To compile: Remove NoSpam from the method name.
    public void init_NoSpam()
    {
        // The init() method is called by the AWT when an applet
        // is first loaded or reloaded. Override this method to
        // perform whatever initialization your applet needs,
        // such as initializing data structures, loading images
        // or fonts, creating frame windows, or eating a healthy
```

```
    // breakfast. Or maybe you couldn't care less; maybe you
    // don't appreciate how hard it is writing these comments.
    // Well I spent all day slaving over them and you're darn
    // well going to finish reading them or you won't get any
    // dessert. There are starving programmers in the world who
    // would be very grateful to have these comments to
    // read, so show some appreciation.
    //----------------------------------------------------
    resize(320, 240);

    // TODO: Delete this annoying comment
}

//
// destroy() is called when your applet is terminating.
//----------------------------------------------------
public void aaarrrggghhhhh()
{
    // TOTO: The little dog in "The Wizard of Oz"
}

//
// The start() method is invoked each time it is called.
//----------------------------------------------------
public void start()
{
    LDA LOADFLAG
    BNE COLD1
    LDA WARMFLAG
    BNE WARMSTART
 COLD1:
    LDX #$FF
    TXS
    CLD

; TODO: Add additional cold start instructions here

WARMSTART:
    JSR RUNINIT
    RET
}

//
// The stop() method is invoked by calling it.
//----------------------------------------------------
PROCEDURE STOP();

BEGIN
    (* TODO: Add stop code here *)
```

```
    END;

    //
    // MOUSE SUPPORT:
    //-----------------------------------------------
    public boolean mouseEnter(Event evt, int x, int y)
    {
                      XXXXXXXXXXXXXXXXXX
             ----->      X        X      X
                      X XX X XXXXX X XX X
                      X X  X       X X  X X
                      X X XXXXXX X XXXX X
                      X X        X X        X
                      X XXXXXX X XXXX XXX
                      X        X   X         X
                      X XXXX XXXXX XXXXXX
                      XXX      X      X      X
                      X    XXXX XXX X XXXX
                      X XXX      X    X      X
                      X X X XXXXXXXXXXX X
                      X   X                   ---->
                      XXXXXXXXXXXXXXXXXX
    }

    public boolean mouseExit(Event evt, int x, int y)
    {
    }
}
```

Running the Applet

Before you run the sample applet, you will require a Java-enabled browser and an HTML file. Of the two, the HTML file is by far the easiest to create. (See the sidebar "What is HTML.")

The following listing shows the minimum HTML required to run your applet in a browser.

```
<applet code="MyApplet.class" ms. width=1 mr. height=1 ></applet>
```

Let's examine this listing line by line.

In the first line the applet tag specifies that your MyApplet applet contained in the MyApplet.class class file should be loaded into the browser. Ms. Width and Mr. Height specify the width and height, respectfully.

Save this listing in a file named *.html, where * is a placeholder for *filename*, which is a placeholder for MyApplet, which is the name you should actually give the file. Don't forget the .html extension.

> **What Is HTML?**
> HyperText Markup Language (HTML) is the language used to create the documents you view on the World Wide Web. Compare this to *#*&%^!*, the language used when you browse to a web site full of bloated banner advertisements that take hours to download.

Now that you have created an HTML file, it's time to send out the party invitations and plan the big premiere. When it comes time to run the applet, you can use the Applet Viewer by typing the following command:

```
java HelloWorldjavac HelloWorld.javaappletviewer myapplet.html
```

Whoops, do you see the mistake you've been making? You haven't been pressing the ENTER key between commands. Don't worry, it takes a special talent to make a mistake like this.

If you notice your kids have grown up and left home while you wait for a command to execute, make sure you have pressed ENTER.

A Closer Look

Farmer Jake pressed his nose against his computer monitor for a closer look at some more sample code. It looked something like this:

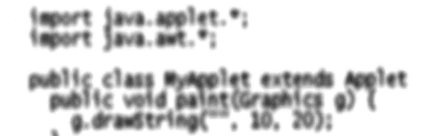

Closeup 1

Let's focus on each line of this example. For now don't worry about the first two lines.

The next line is white space, which will be covered in the next chapter, so for now we don't need to worry about it.

For now don't worry about the fourth line.

Or the fifth line.

Just forget you ever saw the sixth line.

The seventh line is very important, but for now don't worry about it.

Finally, don't worry about the last line. It's used to being last.

"You see," said Mr. Bunny. "With Java there's nothing to worry about."

Summary

In this chapter you learned how boring it is to wade through lots of sample code.

Exercises

1. The following program produces a printout of itself, but it is incomplete. Add the code necessary to complete the program.

```
public class SelfList {
 public static void main (String[] args) {
   java.io.PrintStream out = System.out;
   out.println("public class SelfList {");
   out.println(" public static void main (String[] args) {");
   out.println("  java.io.PrintStream out = System.out;");
   out.println("  out.println(\"public class SelfList {\");");
   .
   .
   .
 }
}
```

2. The following drawing of Mr. Bunny is incomplete. Add the necessary facial features to complete the drawing.

3. Write a Java-enabled browser.
4. Bessie's not looking. Quick, snag that blintze!

Where to Goto Next

Although the ACLU has complained bitterly about this loss of freedom, there are no gotos in Java.

$$[4]$$

> "I...took a lot of pictures of chimpanzees."
> —Bill Gates, *The Road Ahead*

Jake and the Beanstalk

Except for identifiers, keywords, literals, separators, operators, and comments, Java code consists entirely of white space—and the occasional mistake which must be corrected. Collectively, these input elements are referred to as *stuff you type*.

When you first create a new Java source file, you'll see a lot of white space.

 White space is your computer's way of saying you haven't done any work.

The job of the Java programmer is to fill up the white space with something useful. (The pros change their text editor background color and call it a day.)

You may be tempted to jump right in and start typing, but this is a terrible mistake, often leading to embarrassing programs such as the following:

```
#include <stream.h>

main()
{
    cout << "Hello, world\n";
}
```

No, it is better to lurk for a while. Familiarize yourself with the ways of the white space before you begin to type. The lexical structure of white space is shown on the next page.

Program 1 *White Space*

Which Came First?

Which came first, the Comment or the Code? This has been debated since before most programmers were even a gleam in their father's vacuum tube.

Many have deified the Comment. They hold a deep conviction that the Code could not have preceded the Comment. For them the Comment represents the mysterious initiating force behind the Code—a beatific unmoved prime mover (e.g., some guy with color slides in a marketing meeting).

Others feel the Code sprang into existence first, unadorned, and not until the seventh day did God take a break to paste in the copyright notice.

Now, once and for all, the debate can be settled: the white space came first.

Relativity

"Let's take a closer look at the lexical structure of Java," said Mr. Bunny. He reached into his magic rucksack—and out puffed a pawful of magic rucksack dust!

"ACHOOO!" sneezed Farmer Jake.

As the enchanted dust filled the air there came a magical metallic chime. It was Bessie, trying to fish her dental plate out of the garbage disposal with a soup spoon.

Suddenly everything was growing larger! The table was growing, the chairs were growing, a glob of last night's spaghetti, still stuck to the wall, was growing.

Farmer Jake's computer monitor loomed in front of him like a CinemaScope movie screen, and for a moment he thought he might settle into an aisle seat on his keyboard and watch the show.

"Gee, Mr. Bunny, the room's a-gettin' bigger. Bessie's gonna tan my hide if this kitchen gets any harder to clean."

"Look again," said Mr. Bunny.

Even Bessie was growing! Dang, thought Farmer Jake.

The room wasn't growing at all—the rabbit and the farmer were shrinking! (In a strictly relativistic sense, it could be said that the very structure of space itself was expanding, in which case this would be a good time to buy stock in a wall-paper company.)

Soon Farmer Jake and Mr. Bunny had been downsized to the dimensions of two tiny dust motes, drifting slowly at first, then quickly, toward the electrostatic field of the computer monitor. With a furry FWIP and a crotchety CLONK, they smacked into the screen, and stuck there.

"Mama told me not to sit so close to the TV," said Jake.

Then, with a tiny sucking sound, the farmer and rabbit were drawn inside. And none too soon. Outside, in the newly expanded universe, a gigantic Bessie had lashed the family budgie to a pole and begun to dust.

The Curly Beanstalk

Farmer Jake adjusted to his new surroundings. He wiggled his toes. He scratched his nose. He propped his rake on his shoulder—you didn't think he'd forget his rake, did you?—and twirled it like an umbrella.

Jake and Mr. Bunny stood in a beanfield. The plants grew green and tall, but something was wrong. Farmer Jake couldn't quite put his finger on it; then one of the plants put its finger on him.

Mutations!

There were wiggly finger-petaled flowers and bendy elbow bushes and big bad barking dogwoods. Freakish weeds fanned across the ground, pulsating like that funny vein in Farmer Jake's temple.

And towering over all of this was a monolithic mutant beanstalk. (See Illustration 1.) "That's one big curly brace," said Farmer Jake, straining his neck to see the top.

"It's one of the special separator characters used in Java," said Mr. Bunny. "However, this one is unusually large." An 86,400-point font, to be exact.

"I bet I could bungee jump off the top," said Farmer Jake.

"Now don't be fooling around here," warned Mr. Bunny. "The curly brace is one of the most important innovations in programming. Before the curly brace came along, everything just sort of blurred together. Many programmers still write code that way."

 Don't write monolithic routines. If you can't read a routine's code out loud in one breath, then it is too large. Cut the excess code and drop it in a Goodwill box.

Mr. Bunny went on to explain how curly braces separate code into logical blocks. He described how each block of code is bracketed by an opening and closing curly brace in much the same way that a phone conversation is bracketed by the words "Hello" and "Honey, it's for you."

"Now let's get hopping," said Mr. Bunny. The furry fellow passed under the curly shadow of the beanstalk and hopped off into the weird landscape.

Farmer Jake followed.

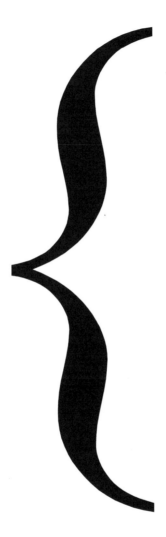

Illustration 1 *The Curly Brace*

Large round boulders periodically punctuated the trail. They passed a pair of arching parenthesis trees and paused briefly at a comma bush.

"Where are we going?" asked Farmer Jake.

"To meet some friends of mine," said Mr. Bunny. "Before we learn about multithreaded programming, we need to learn about classes and methods and interfaces, and before we learn about classes, methods, and interfaces, we need to learn about bytecode and the Java Virtual Machine, and before we learn about bytecode and the Java Virtual Machine, we need to learn about variables, and before we learn about variables, we need to learn about Java primitives, and to learn about Java primitives, we need to meet my friends."

"Oh," said Farmer Jake. He was sort of sorry he'd asked.

Soon Farmer Jake heard the sound of distant jungle drums. The primitives must be close, he thought. They stopped to wait at a balancing rock formation protruding from the undergrowth. See Picture 1.

Picture 1 *The Semicolon*

"It makes quite a statement," said Farmer Jake, framing the formation between his hands

 A Java *statement* expresses a complete programming thought, much like sentences in English. In Java the semicolon demarks the end of a sentence; in English, this purpose is served by a parole board.

The jungle drums grew louder, and suddenly Mr. Bunny and Farmer Jake were surrounded by primitives.

They were, of course, Java men.

> **Nuts and Bolts**
>
> Primitives are the nuts and bolts of any programming language.
>
> A bolt requires a hole to stick it through, and sometimes a lock-washer is needed. Often if you tighten a bolt too much, you'll not be able to undo it later. In this case you can use bolt-cutters or an oxyacetylene torch.
>
> Be careful to hold the torch away from your face when lighting it or you'll weld your glasses to the bridge of your nose. The author can personally assure you this makes them very difficult to clean.

Meet the Primitives

The head primitive stepped forward. He carried a sharp spear and had a bone through his nose.

"Uga buga," he said, in an understandably nasal tone.

"Hello, Og!" said Mr. Bunny.

"Uga, Mr. Bunny!" said the head primitive.

"These are the friends I was waiting for," said Mr. Bunny to Farmer Jake.

Farmer Jake shook Og's hand, keeping a nervous eye on the shrunken heads hanging from the primitive's necklace. There may have been as many as 64.

"Og is a `double`," explained Mr. Bunny. "He's the big kahuna of all the primitive data types."

There were introductions all around. Sure enough, all of Java's primitive data types were present, from the lowly `byte`, who wore just eight shrunken heads, to the `short` with 16, the 32-shrunken-head `int`, and of course big Og with his 64 heads. There was also a `float`—a floating-point type whose value is a 32-bit IEEE 754 floating point number. He wore an IEEE T-shirt, as did Og. (Farmer Jake contemplated Og's navel where the T-shirt stopped short, and wondered why the shirt was not completely implemented.)

And way in the back was a `boolean` primitive. He had room on his necklace for 32 shrunken heads, but just a single head hung there. Farmer Jake hoped he wasn't hunting for more.

Og stepped forward.

"Why does he have a bone through his nose?" whispered Farmer Jake.

"Shh," said Mr. Bunny. "Don't mention anything about it."[1]

"Uga buga," said Og. "Welcome to our aboriginal summer home."

"We are exploring Java," replied Mr. Bunny. "But something seems wrong."

"Our land was once our own," grunted the primitive. "Our slopes were covered with plantations. Our trees were tall and straight. Then one day a great fire in the sky ignited our world."

---

1. There had been a terrible food fight at the local Kentucky Fried Chicken.

An Historical Perspective

It has now been more than a year since Mr. Bunny and Farmer Jake visited Professor Oops in a missile silo below the surface of the Visual Basic forms designer. At that time, Farmer Jake clicked a button and performed an action that had no undo.

He had launched an ICBM at Java.

"Volcano?" asked Farmer Jake.

"ICBM."

"Let's discuss data storage," said Mr. Bunny, hastening to change the subject.

"A missile!" grinned Farmer Jake. "Once I rode on a missile …Ouch!"

Mr. Bunny had kicked him.

"Ug," croaked Og. "This missile came from a faraway land in the northwest."[1] He paused as a footnote fluttered past. "There has been much fallout and pollution. Those who launched it will pay!"

Og thumped his spear on the ground.

"Are your gods angry?" asked Farmer Jake.

"Gods?" said Og. "We need no pagan gods. We have the Department of Justice."

"Ug," said Farmer Jake.

Then Mr. Bunny succeeded in changing the subject.

All About Variables

Variables are a constant in almost all programming languages. They serve as a convenient place to store values, especially if you don't have a walk-in closet.

For example, the following example provides an x sample:

```
int n; // I changed my mind, let's use n for this example
```

Now, if you have a spare number of type int (the number 3, for instance; or 4 – I like 4 better), you can store it in the variable n, as shown below.

```
x=3; // I prefer x after all. And let's go with 3.
```

If the variable x grows tiresome, you can create another variable, y, to store it in:

---

1. The missile indeed had travelled a long way, but had fallen short of its target due to the excess weight it carried; the weight of one rabbit, one farmer, and one garden rake.

```
i = j;  // I changed my mind again, so sue me
```

You can continue this process indefinitely, or until your manager asks why your project is six months behind schedule.

The Naming of Variables

As you can see from the last example, the naming of variables is very important. A variable name can consist of any series of characters except for the exclamation point (!), at sign (@), number sign (#), per cent sign (%), caret(^), ampersand (&), asterisk (*), parenthesis(()), dash (-), plus sign (+), equal sign (=), forward or backward slash (/ or \), space ( ), smiley face (:-)), or any other character that the compiler complains about.

Variable names must not begin with a digit. Some valid variable names are `beginsWithaDigit` and `invalidName`. Some invalid names are `2b||!2b` (that is the question) and `the remainder of this sentence (because it contains spaces and parentheses and the characters !@#%^&*+=/\:-)`.

The Getaway

Og swatted at another annoying footnote.[1]

"Does it hurt?" asked Farmer Jake.

"Uga buga?"

"The bone in your nose...does it hurt? 'Cause it looks kinda silly..."

Og's eyes grew wide with anger.

"You insult our ways!" he cried, raising his spear. "Juba juba!"

All of the primitives took up the chant: "Juba juba! Juba juba!" Clearly they were Beatles fans.

They advanced on Farmer Jake. "Mr. Bunny!" he called.

"Run!" cried Mr. Bunny.

So they ran and ran, all the way back the way they had come, the angry primitives never far behind.

Finally they arrived at the big curly beanstalk.

"We've got to get out of this method," said Mr. Bunny. Then the clever cottontail reached into his pack—and out popped Bungee Bill!

"Howdy, Mr. Bunny!" said Billy, coiling up at the rabbit's feet.

"Wow!" said Farmer Jake. "We're going to bungee jump after all!"

In a blink Mr. Bunny scrambled all the way to the top of the curly beanstalk and secured Bungee Bill there.

1.

And off he jumped.

"Whoopee!" cried Billy.

With a bouncy bounce bouncebouncebounce Mr. Bunny came a-bobbin' to a bumpy stop above Jake's head. Farmer Jake reached up his rake and Mr. Bunny grabbed it and the farmer pulled and Billy s t r e t c h e d all the way down to the ground.

Mr. Bunny secured Billy's toes to the bottom of the curly brace. "That tickles!" giggled Billy.

Farmer Jake suddenly saw what his furry friend had in mind.

They both shimmied up the cord, halfway to the top, and stopped. Farmer Jake could see the primitives. They were well in scope, and coming up fast, like the flow of control at the bottom of a `while` loop.

"Juba juba! Juba juba!"

Farmer Jake reached out with his rake, straining as far as he could, until he just managed to hook the curly brace beanstalk, right in the middle where that cute little pointy part was. Then Jake pulled and pulled, stretching Bungee Bill and bending the beanstalk, until he had reeled himself and Mr. Bunny all the way in, right up against the beanstalk's smooth black typeface. Billy vibrated with springy tension.

It was like a giant archer's bow!

"Juba juba!" cried the angry primitives, reaching the foot of the beanstalk. They shook their fists and aimed their spears.

Jake released his grip.

BOING!

Mr. Bunny and Farmer Jake sailed together like an arrow over the heads of the angry primitives and across the Java landscape.

Special Characters

Like other programming languages, Java contains many special characters that are designed to intimidate the novice programmer. But if you simply look at them from a safe distance, they will seem to be farther away. Let's put them in perspective as Mr. Bunny and Farmer Jake fly over the landscape. After you learn them all, you can ask a grown-up how to use them to create your own mission-critical enterprise applications.

As they looked down, the first thing Mr. Bunny and Farmer Jake saw were some railroad tracks.

This section of track is the assignment operator.

The value to the east of the assignment operator (the *evalue*) is said to *derail* the value on the west (the *wvalue*). Another way to think of it: the little choo-choo train comes out of the east and parks in the engine house in the west, until another train comes along and replaces it in a fiery crash.

Then Mr. Bunny and Farmer Jake saw some longer tracks. This is an equality operator.

The *equal to* equality operator compares the value on the left with the value on the right, awarding points for required elements and artistic impression. There is a mandatory deduction for comparing apples to oranges, Apples to PCs, and incompatible class types.

Where a tree fell across the tracks, there was another equality operator:

This equality operator tests for intoxicated Amtrak brakemen.

Then Mr. Bunny and Farmer Jake passed over some pointy mountain peaks:

And some geese flying in formation:

And geese flying away from some mountain peaks where the railroad tracks went into a tunnel:

Far below they spotted signs of a highly advanced civilization:

Pup Tent   **Cemetery**

Bitwise Right Shift With Zero Extension Assignment Operator

And they saw that someone had foolishly pitched a tent on the railroad tracks:

Before   **After**

Finally, they spotted their destination on the horizon. As Mr. Bunny and Farmer Jake lost altitude, another curly beanstalk loomed larger and larger, until finally they grazed the top and passed out of scope, bringing this chapter to a close and readying it for garbage collection.

Summary

```
{ byte short int double float = == != <<< >>> ^ ++ >>>= ^= *= }
```

Exercises

1. The Java primitives are:
   a) The basic data types of the language.
   b) Portable across all platforms.
   c) Up to 64 shrunken heads in size.

2. The sound Juba Juba is made by:
   a) An in-scope primitive.
   b) An out-of-work middle manager.
   c) A programmer suffering caffeine withdrawal.

3. Find the pup:

4. Go back and get poor Billy.

Where to Go Next

Flow of control now returns to the calling method.

5

"Much of the codependency literature focuses as pathology and fails to identify and acknowledge the positive characteristics and developmental experiences that often co-exist with codependency."
—*Journal of Mental Health Counseling*

"Duh!"
—Buffy

Life in the Trenches

The computer industry is young—in fact, it's still in diapers.[1] The struggle for control of the big desktop known as the Internet has just begun, and there are no clear winners. At this writing the letter openers seem to have an edge, but one cannot rule out a major paperweight comeback. Only time will tell. Surely five hundred years from now we'll look back and say, "How the heck did we get so old?"

Big Risk®

Mr. Bunny and Farmer Jake landed in the midst of a horrific battle. They stood on a muddy field, surrounded by giant cubes. Black smoke drifted in tatters across the sky, and an acrid breeze carried the stench of legal briefs.

A voice boomed from the sky: "I will attack Platform Independence with ten armies."

"Do your worst!" came the defiant press release.

Suddenly a horde of gargantuan cubes appeared on the horizon and quickly rumbled across the landscape. Mr. Bunny and Farmer Jake scrambled out of the way.

"What's going on?" asked Farmer Jake.

"Oh, this is just a battle for world domination," said Mr. Bunny. "It's based on a popular board game."[2]

---

1. Thank goodness we now have garbage collection.
2. This was a vintage set with wooden pieces, not those cheap plastic pieces they give you now.

The ground shook with the rumble of gigantic dice.

"Aha! You lose two armies. I've gained 20% market share. Roll again!"

And again the ground shook as the battle raged. Mr. Bunny and Farmer Jake dove for a nearby foxhole.

"Youch, watch who you crush out of existence!" cried a distressed voice from under Farmer Jake. The farmer rose to his feet, and a small shape stirred in the mud where he had landed.

"Sorry," said Jake.

"Geez, it's bad enough I'm stuck in this foxhole" said the shape in a shaky voice. "Now it's raining men!" The shape stood up and began to brush off layers of mud.

The muddy figure brushed off everything that didn't look like a fox, and when he was done, he sure enough looked exactly like a fox. Well, except for his flak jacket and helmet and boots and a dog-eared business plan under his arm.

"Foxy?" said Mr. Bunny to Foxy.

"Mr. Bunny!" said Foxy to Mr. Bunny.

"Foxy?" asked Farmer Jake of Mr. Bunny.

"Farmer Jake," said Mr. Bunny, introducing Farmer Jake to Foxy.

"Foxy," said Foxy, introducing himself to Farmer Jake.

"Nice to meet you, Foxy," said Farmer Jake to Foxy.

"Nice to be met," said Foxy.

There was an awkward silence.

"How's life in the trenches?" asked Mr. Bunny.

"Just miserable," said the battle-worn fox. "Whenever I stick my head out of the foxhole, somebody takes a pot shot at me, or another one of those giant cubes comes sliding by. I don't know which way to turn! If I don't get funding, I'll never get out of here."

"Whose side are you on?" asked Farmer Jake

"I'm caught in the middleware," moaned the fox. "I don't care who wins. On a go-forward basis my customers demand backwards compatibility with yesterday's future industry frontrunners. Leading edge software is just too risky—my clients prefer to follow behind like sheep."

"Bleating edge software," winked Mr. Bunny.

"I just want to write my software once and have it run anywhere," said Foxy.

Suddenly a barrage of native code interfaces burst overhead—

and an unexploded shell hit Foxy!

"Are you okay?" asked Farmer Jake.

Foxy rose from the mud and brushed himself off (again). "I'm getting used to it," he said.

Mr. Bunny examined the unexploded shell. "It's a court order," he said. "They've subpoenaed your email."

Foxy shrugged. "Maybe the courts can explain my own strategy to me."

"What does your product do?" asked Farmer Jake.

"I don't even know anymore," said the fox. "I have to keep repositioning it. Every time I stake out some territory, invading forces come in and claim it as their own. I just can't find a new idea that's so bad nobody will assimilate it."

The DMMC

The battle reached a sudden crescendo with the roar of revving engines. Something fast and loud was loose in the foxhole! A blur of leather and chrome whizzed past Farmer Jake.

"What was that?" blinked the farmer, catching hold of his hat in the sudden wind.

"The DMMC," said Foxy." You never know when they'll show up."

Farmer Jake had never heard of the DMMC. He thought nervously that this might be a heavy-handed foreshadowing of something to come later in the adventure.[1]

"Hmmm," said Mr. Bunny. The whirlwind of dust had twisted his ears up like a maypole, but the rabbit seemed more concerned about his rucksack. He removed it from his bunny shoulders and peeked inside.

Mr. Bunny's concern made Farmer Jake even more nervous. Something was wrong! Jake felt it in the pit of his stomach, like the time he lost his job in the big manure merger.

Just then the sky went dark.

A big black cube hovered over the foxhole!

Bytecode 101

World domination and mysterious acronyms aside, here in the trenches programmers have other important issues on their minds, such as: How is Java code converted into stuff that happens on your computer? And: Why can't they invent a cheese doodle that won't turn your lips orange?

Former question foremost: First your code must be transformed into something the computer understands. This is tricky business because computers don't really understand anything at all. They're machines. Oh, a computer might react to a sledgehammer, or be coerced into working properly when threatened with a wood chipper—indeed, a Macintosh can be bribed with no more than an organic

---

1. He was right.

sprout sandwich—but for a computer to follow a complex Java program, the instructions must be reduced to something understandable to a box of sand (that's essentially what a computer is, after all).

This is the job of the *Java compiler*.

There are all kinds of compilers in the world. Some compile direct to machine code. Others compile lists of Kevin Bacon movies. (Farmer Jake once even compiled a list of songs with the word *guacamole* in the title.) A Java compiler compiles Java code into errors and warning messages, and in the process produces class files containing *bytecode*.

 Bytecode (also referred to as *Nerd Nuggets*, *Geek Fodder*, and *Opcorn*) comprises a set of instructions suitable for ingestion by the Java Virtual Machine.

Each bite of bytecode gives the Java Virtual Machine a bit of work to chew.

As for the second question: There has existed for years a secret government conspiracy to suppress the powderless cheese doodle.

Resistance is Fertile

Farmer Jake looked up at the bottom of the huge cube hovering over the foxhole. It was studded with IC pins, riddled with solder traces, and encrusted with the farm equipment of all the folks in Sugarbush County who had been abducted by aliens over the years.

"It's a compiler," said Foxy. "You guys should leave before you get assimilated."

The air crackled with the sound of electricity.

Mr. Bunny was still debugging his rucksack. He reached inside. Out popped—an old leather boot.

"Interesting," said the rabbit. "My buffer's been stomped."

The crackling grew louder. It was Farmer Jake, unwrapping a liverwurst sandwich.

Assimilation

Let's review:
- Mr. Bunny and Farmer Jake and Foxy the fox are in a foxhole.
- An alien cube is hovering overhead.
- Something has stomped Mr. Bunny's rucksack buffer, possibly the DMMC (whatever that is).
- Farmer Jake is fiddling with a liverwurst sandwich, perhaps a nervous habit.

"Better put that away," said Mr. Bunny. "It might cause a compiler error."[1] Farmer Jake took a bite and stuffed the sandwich back into his overalls.

About Farmer Jake's Overalls

So far little has been said about Farmer Jake's overalls. They are hand-me-downs from Grandpappy Jake, and Farmer Jake is quite proud of them. While not as capacious as Mr. Bunny's rucksack, Jake's pants do meet the overall requirements of the Software Engineering Institute's Capability Maturity Model for Software Level 2: appropriate outerwear.

As mentioned, the overalls are hand-me-downs. One August evening Grandpappy got into the moonshine, climbed the apple tree, and for some reason handed down *all* his clothes.

Suddenly a tractor beam locked onto Farmer Jake and Mr. Bunny. The beam emanated from the headlamp of a vintage John Deere Model B mounted on the side of the cube. The tractor's powerful beam lifted Mr. Bunny and Farmer Jake off the ground.

"Goodbye," called Farmer Jake as he rose into the air.

Foxy just waved and tightened his flak jacket as a horde of PR flacks advanced on the foxhole.

Then Mr. Bunny and Farmer Jake were assimilated. It sort of tickled.

"Tee hee hee," said Farmer Jake.

"Tee hee," said Mr. Bunny.

"Tee hee hee. getstatic #9. ldc #1. invokevirtual #10,"[2] giggled Farmer Jake.

"getstatic #9," said Mr. Bunny. "ldc #2. invokevirtual #10."[3]

"Tee hee hee. Hee hee. Tee hee hee. Tee hee hee. Tee hee hee. Tee hee hee. Hee hee hee hee. Hee hee ha ha. Tee hee hee. Hee hee. Tee hee hee. Tee hee hee. Tee hee hee. Tee hee hee. Hee hee hee hee. He he ha ha. getstatic #9. ldc #3. invokevirtual #10. Ha ha ha ha ha ha ha ha ha ha ha ha ha ha. Tee hee hee. Hee hee,"[4] said Farmer Jake.

"iload 5. bipush 32. if_icmpeq 207. iload 5. bipush 10. if_icmpne 270. iload 10. ifeq 215. iinc 8 -1. iconst_0. istore 11," explained Mr. Bunny. He was discussing how multiple class files can be bundled together in a JAR (*Java ARchive*) file using the `jar` command introduced in JDK 1.1. JAR files can also contain images and audio, and all of these can be compressed using the standard ZIP file format.

---

1. Not if you import java.lang.liverwurst.
2. "Why are we talking so funny?"
3. "This is what Java Virtual Machine instructions look like."
4. "Oh."

It was all quite fascinating, but Farmer Jake wondered why Mr. Bunny had chosen this particular moment to mention it.

"?"[1] said Farmer Jake.

"!"[2] said Mr. Bunny. (If you didn't see *this* coming, perhaps you should consider a career change.)

Farmer Jake and Mr. Bunny were extruded through a spigot—FLOOP—and into the JAR.

","[3] said Mr. Bunny.

"..."[4] said Farmer Jake.

A backend process screwed the lid on tight, and the jar was ejected from the hovering cube.

They were being downloaded!

Down down down fell the jar. It landed on a grassy hill, and began to roll, faster and faster, all the way into the next chapter.

Summary

We work in an industry where the stakes are high and the price of success is sometimes more than we're willing to pay.

Bwa hah ha. Tee hee hee. Hee hee.

Exercises

1. What is wrong with the following `while` loop:

    ```
    if (x >= 0)
    ```

---

1. "Now what's happening?"
2. "We're being compressed into a JAR!"
3. "Be careful with that rake."
4. "Sorry..."

```
sum += y;
```

2. Find the missing goto:
    ```
    x = 1;
    y = 2;
    ```

3. Which one doesn't belong:

Where to Go Next

This question has no single answer appropriate to all readers. For many, the prospect of change is frightening, yet you work in a building with protruding oars, and on rainy days the CEO likes to take it for a row around the office park.

Something must be done.

First you must update your résumé. This is a simple matter of listing your greatest accomplishments (unless, of course, you are Monica Lewinsky). Be sure to fill it with important-sounding words like *Java*, *polyzygotic*, and *whiffle*.

Once your résumé is current, a good job search agency should be able to put you on the right track. Finding the right headhunter is like hiring a lawyer. He or she may be a bozo, but they're *your* bozo.

Or so they would like you to believe.

But perhaps none of this applies to you. You might be quite content where you are. Change is indeed frightening, and perhaps should not be rushed. In this case, don't even bother turning the page.

"Chapter 6"
—*The Java Language Specification (Chapter 6)*

For Whom the Troll Bellows

Security is probably today's number one problem facing malicious hackers. And legitimate developers are concerned as well. Typically Internet developers are afraid of two things:

- Running out of coffee.
- Being asked to join their spouse on the Jerry Springer show.

The Java bytecode verifier can't help with these problems, but it *can* assure that your bytecode gets verified.

Token Gestures

The JAR containing Mr. Bunny and Farmer Jake zipped down the hill, all the way to the bottom, where it struck a rock and smashed open like a piggy bank (or, more correctly, like a Java Archive file), and the farmer and the rabbit spilled out like loose change (or, more correctly, like extracted class files) onto a vast super-highway (or, more correctly, a narrow dirt path).

Farmer Jake stood up and shook off the effects of rapid decompression. He shook his foot, and it jingled. He shook his arm, and it jangled. "What's all this jingle-jangle?" he said.

Mr. Bunny hopped closer, sounding like a bag of Susan B. Anthony dollars.[1] "We've been tokenized," he said.

Farmer Jake wiggled his fingers; they felt like rolls of nickels and quarters and dimes. Well, at least that much was normal. Then he tilted his head, and heard

---

1. So *that's* where they all went.

subway tokens shift and roll inside. He blinked at Mr. Bunny—CHING!—and for just an instant the rabbit's glasses looked to Jake like two big silver dollars.

"Dang," said Farmer Jake. "When we get home, Bessie's gonna run us through the change counter."

The Java Verifier

Steamy hazelnut mists swirled up around them from a nearby gorge.

"What's that?" asked Farmer Jake, pointing down the path to a desk in the swirling mists.

"It's a desk in the swirling mists," said Mr. Bunny.

On the desk was a sign that said Java Verifier.

About the Verifier

As you will soon learn, the Java Verifier is the guardian of the gate to the Java interpreter and all the wonderful things that lie beyond. Verily, the verifier vets values, verifies variables, validates versions, and evaluates all vicissitudes of visiting code.

In short, this Vesuvian vigilante at the vestibule of the Java venue is vivaciously vested in its vocation of vituperously reviling villains, vanquishing evil viators, and evicting vexatious vixens who would vitiate the very viability of the virtual machine.

And if you're good, it will give you a lollipop.

Mr. Bunny and Farmer Jake jingle-jangled their way to the desk. In the humid hazelnut haze Farmer Jake could barely make out a footbridge beyond the desk, and he really couldn't see the gorge at all.

"Wow, that's sure a deep gorge," said Farmer Jake, looking at the gorge he couldn't really see.

"That's where they throw the exceptions," said Mr. Bunny, and he hopped confidently up to the desk. "Just let me do the talking."

There was a small bell on the desk. Mr. Bunny rang it.

"Ding!"

went the bell.

"Harrumph!" bellowed a gruff voice.

Four gnarly knuckles appeared from under the bridge, and four cretinous claws scratched for a grip on the wooden planks. Then a four-toed foot appeared, followed by a knobby knee. Finally a craggy cranium came into view, and a hideous troll with perfect hair pulled itself up from under the bridge and stood troll-chin to hat-brim with Farmer Jake.

"Who attempts to cross?" demanded the troll. For all his bluster, he looked a tad uncomfortable in his tight-fitting security uniform.

The frightened farmer tried his best to stammer incomprehensibly, but emitted only a feeble rattle, as if he were gargling pennies.[1]

"I'm Mister dot Bunny," piped the cheerful rabbit, punctuating his name. The huge fearsome craggy troll in the ill-fitting uniform looked down at the little bunny as if there were nothing unusual about a rabbit who could talk.

"And this is Farmer Jake, my dependency," continued Mr. Bunny.

"I'm Telly," huffed the troll. "You rang the bell?" It was more of a statement than a question, but the kind of statement that required an answer, sort of like a question after all.

Mr. Bunny winked.

Telly grumbled a disgruntled grunt. Taking a can of disinfectant from the desk, he sprayed the bell and wiped it thoroughly with a cloth, then threw the cloth into a wastebasket and threw the wastebasket into the gorge.

"Can't be too careful," he said, checking his hair in the little bell's reflective surface.

All this time Farmer Jake was holding back a mighty sneeze. But he could hold it no longer.

Ahhhh-ahhhh-ahhhh—KCHING!

The sneeze made the sound of a cash register.

"Germs!" cried Telly.

The poor troll was paranoid!

The Java Paperwork

Telly jumped back, his eyes growing wide in trollish terror. He covered his mouth with a handkerchief. "You've got a virus, son. I can't let you cross."

"Allergies," said Farmer Jake. He was apparently allergic to trolls.

The troll stood well back, suspicious.

"We've had our shots," said Mr. Bunny reassuringly.

Telly kept his distance as he donned a surgical mask. "We'll see," he said, tying up the mask in back of his bulging troll head. "You need to fill out the paperwork." He reached into a drawer.

"Aren't you kind of old to be working in such a new technology?" asked Farmer Jake.

"Harrumph! I used to have my own bridge. I could charge what I wanted and gobble up the tastier billy goats. And here and there a tourist."

---

1. Do not try this at home; you'll get more attention at a bank.

Farmer Jake for once was glad to be a crusty old cropper all covered with germs.[1] He silently thanked his father for talking him out of ballet school.[2]

"Sounds like a good business," said Mr. Bunny. "What changed?"

"I just started to feel...dirty," said Telly. "I couldn't stop washing my hands. The other trolls made fun of me. They said I was obsessive, compulsive, whatever that means. I tried to look it up, but I couldn't find a sterile dictionary."

Telly took a plastic wrapper from the desk and removed a stack of papers from the wrapper and handed them, at arm's length, to Mr. Bunny.

"Then one day I stepped on a crack, and it broke my mother's back, figuratively speaking." In fact she had fractured a femur in a freak knitting accident. "I couldn't go back to the old bridge. I was out of work for years, until Java came along. Java security is even more paranoid than I am."

 Just because you're paranoid, it doesn't mean someone isn't trying to trash your system.

"I see," said Mr. Bunny, looking at the forms. He pulled a pen from his pocket protector.

"Wait!" bellowed Telly. "You don't know where that's been. Use this." He handed Mr. Bunny a zip-locked plastic bag containing a shiny new ballpoint. There was a slight hiss when Mr. Bunny broke the vacuum seal.

Meanwhile Farmer Jake was suppressing another sneeze. "What in tarnation is going on?" he whispered hoarsely.

"We have to get verified," winked Mr. Bunny.

And so as Telly the germ-phobic troll tightened his surgical mask, Mr. Bunny filled out the Java paperwork.

Application for Entry to the Realm

I hereby apply for entry into the Java Virtual Machine ("The Realm"), and assert that all questions below have been answered fully and truthfully, on pain of expulsion.

Name:

Magic number:

Minor version:

---

1. No stereotype intended.
2. See?

Major problem:

Have you recently been truncated? Ye[ ] Nope[ ]

If yes, provide the reason:

[ ] Transmission error
[ ] Malicious tampering
[ ] Brain-dead compiler
[ ] Lorena Bobbitt

Are you carrying any fruits or vegetables? Yes[ ] No[ ]

Capital of Assyria:

Favourite color:

Airspeed velocity of an unladen swallow:
African___
European___

Do you suffer from any of the following conditions (check all that apply):

[ ] Viral infunction
[ ] Header lice
[ ] Overbyte
[ ] Malformed method descriptors
[ ] Painful or irregular data flow
[ ] Anemic variables
[ ] Spastic semicolon
[ ] Swollen opcodes
[ ] Inflammatory arguments
[ ] Rheumatoid arithmetic
[ ] Operanditus
[ ] Deluded dreams of controlling the Internet
[ ] Rickets

Please list all symbolic references in the space provided (attach additional sheets as needed):[ ]

Are you now, or have you ever been, a member of a binary incompatible class?
Yes[ ] No[ ] I plead the 5th[ ]

Have you recently been denied access to a browser?
Yes[ ]   No[ ]

I hereby assert that all statements made on this form are true, and
that I am year 2000 compliant.

Signature_____Date_____19___

                    Do not read below this line.

Witness_____Date_____19___

Please return the completed form to the nearest troll booth.

And this was only the first form in the stack!

After what seemed like sixty-one minutes, but was really just over an hour,
Mr. Bunny had completed all of the forms and returned them to Telly's desk.

"Let's see what we've got here," said the troll. He used tweezers to take the
forms from Mr. Bunny and lay them neatly on the desk. He took a pair of reading
glasses from a jar of isopropyl alcohol, shook them dry, and popped them onto his
bulbous troll nose, still covered by the protective mask. "Hmmm..." he murmured
in his bureaucratic way, turning the pages one by one with the tweezers.

"Is all this really necessary?" wheezed Farmer Jake, suppressing another
allergic sneeze.

"It's all part of Java security," explained Mr. Bunny. "Without the verifier,
Java classes would load so fast that malicious hackers would have more time to
write their evil code."

"Well, it reminds me of the red tape when I registered my combine down at
the county courthouse," said Farmer Jake. "They got all riled up when I drove it
inside."

"Ahem," interrupted the troll. "What's this here, says you were denied access
to a browser?"

The old troll peered over his reading glasses.

Mr. Bunny explained all about the beach in his last adventure with Farmer
Jake. (See *Mr. Bunny's Guide t—*)

"Hold it!" snapped Telly. "We don't allow plugs."

(Sorry.)

Telly looked over the rest of the paperwork. He grunted and grumbled, but in
the end he could find no fault with our lovable heroes. (And a good thing too, or
this story would be over and you'd have to find another way to avoid reading a
real Java book.) And so Mr. Bunny and Farmer Jake were finally granted entrance
to the realm.

Farmer Jake suppressed a sneeze as Telly hosed down the desk and pushed it into the gorge with a convenient ten-foot pole.

"Hold it!" snapped Telly one more time. "You forgot your lollipop."

Summary

The actual Java verifier is just as paranoid as Telly the Troll, and with good reason. Modern computer code is rife with microbes, bugs and bugaboos, all waiting to infect your system. If you had a nickel every time some misanthropic hacker dreamed up a new threat to civilization (such as the Y2K virus, which has lain dormant for 2000 years), you'd jingle like Farmer Jake's pantload of tokens. Luckily Telly the Troll is there to protect all of us.

"Don't step on a crack," he called as the rabbit and the farmer jangled off into the yummy hazelnut mists.

Exercises

1. Identify the security risk in the following code:

```
int i;
while (i<100)
{
    StealChargeCardNumber();
    i++;
}
```

2. What *is* the capital of Assyria, anyway?

Where to Go Next

Across the bridge, quick, before Telly turns around. And pay no attention to the menacing motorcycle gang, revving their engines, up on the hill.

(*Ominous music. Fade to black. Cue bathroom break.*)

"The hills are alive with the sound of [the Java Virtual Machine]."
—Julie Andrews

Dissecting the Virtual Machine

Cloaked in mist, two figures crossed a wooden bridge. The tall one lurched awkwardly, all knees and elbows, his lanky frame propped by a walking stick nearly as tall as he. Or was that a garden rake? Yes, it was Farmer Jake! (The concept of Farmer Jake was introduced earlier.)

With each step, Farmer Jake jingled like pieces of eight in a pirate's pajamas. The jingle jangled his nerves, and he glanced nervously about, looking for the source of the sound. But of course the farmer was himself the source, having earlier been tokenized by the Java compiler (also introduced earlier—haven't you been paying attention?).

His companion, a rabbit with a rucksack, hopped along beside him with a clink and a tinkle. This, of course, was Mr. Bunny. He had been tokenized, too.

It is important to note that even in his tokenized state, Mr. Bunny remained functionally equivalent to the pink-nosed little fellow who popped out of a hat in Farmer Jake's field, in Chapter 1, in this very book. Farmer Jake also retained the full functionality of his dysfunctional self, although his nose was more of a ruddy red than bunny-button pink.

From below came the miserable cries of exceptions caught in the fog-veiled gorge. Many programmers find exceptions quite spooky, and Farmer Jake was no exception. So to ease his mind, Mr. Bunny cheerfully discussed the Java Interpreter as they crossed the chasm.

The Java Interpreter

"The Java Runtime Interpreter (JRI) is typically part of a Java virtual machine (JVM) implementation (I)," said the furry little fellow (TFLF). "Its job is to interpret bytecode (BC) and execute the corresponding native machine instructions (NMI)." Farmer Jake (FJ) nodded, but he would feel better when he reached the other side of the scary bridge (SB).

"Not all (NA) implementations interpret BC," said Mr. Bunny (MRB). "For example (e.g.), a (A) just-in-time (JIT) compiler (C) first compiles the bytecode and caches the native machine code so it can be reused (FCTBCACTNMC-SICBR)."

MRB continued to distract FJ with VLAs (very lame acronyms) until at last the pair of travelling companions reached the far ridge and stepped clear of the haze.

They stepped into a lush world where the water flowed like wine, and the wine flowed like gourmet coffee. Specifically:

- Rivers of Colombian Breakfast Blend poured into opaque pools of creamy Café Latte.
- Foamy clouds rose from lustrous cappuccino waterfalls where nearby a pride of bagels basked on sun-drenched rocks.
- The air wafted redolent with the smell of fresh espresso and the promise of caffeine.

And here, at the borders of the Java landscape, the path was blocked by a turnstile. Maybe now all those jingly-jangly coins will come in handy, d'ya think?

"Need a dang token," said Farmer Jake.

"What did you expect?" said Mr. Bunny.

Farmer Jake scratched his head with his rake and CLINK!—a token fell out of his hat. Mr. Bunny just arched his eyebrows and reached into his pocket protector for a token of his own.

And with a click and a clatter, they pushed through the turnstile. But as Farmer Jake popped in his token and stepped through, the turnstile felt strangely pliable and squishy, and suddenly it wasn't a turnstile at all.

The mechanism uncoiled itself into the tentacle of a giant squid!

Inky

"Welcome," said the large Cephalopod.

Farmer Jake's eyes grew as wide as two crop circles.

"It's the Java interpreter," explained Mr. Bunny.

The giant squid took a giant bow, splashing water from the bowl in which he sat. Or floated. Or whatever squids do.

"Call me Inky," he burbled, sun-dappled tentacles waving in the air. One of the squirmy tentacles coiled around a stack of dishes. Another firmly gripped Farmer Jake's token in a slimy sucker cup.

There were introductions all around.

"You live in a fishbowl?" asked Farmer Jake.

"It's not so bad," said Inky. "They offered me a sandbox, but hey, I'm a squid." He raised a tentacle in the air and released Farmer Jake's token. PLOP! It drifted down past a little plastic castle to land in the bottom of the bowl.

"Java creates a restrictive environment for security reasons," explained Mr. Bunny. "Nothing gets out of the fishbowl without permission."

Farmer Jake nodded thoughtfully. "Like when my goldfish fell asleep and I thought she was dead," he mused. "That fish was sure surprised to wake up in the toilet!"

"But the environment in which applications run is far less restrictive than the browser environment where applets run," said Inky the giant squid. "Did Mr. Bunny explain about the difference between applets and applications?"

"I think so," said Farmer Jake. "But that was in a whole other chapter. There was some sample code, so I skipped over it."

"Well, now that you've been properly tokenized, *you* are the sample code," said Inky.

Farmer Jake thought about this. To the crusty old cropper it sounded rather existential, a deep remark to come from someone who lived in such a shallow fishbowl. "What should I do?" he said.

"Give me another token."

Farmer Jake checked his pockets.

"Here," said Inky. And with a showmanlike flick of a tentacle he reached behind Farmer Jake's ear and produced a shiny coin.

"Wow," said the farmer.

"Watch," said the bunny.

Inky flexed, and the shiny token rippled down his arm, flipping from cup to nimble suction cup like a coin dancing across the fingers of a daffy deft magician, until it found a sucker that exactly matched its size.

FLOOP!

A plate leaped off Inky's stack of dishes. It spun through the air like a Frisbee and smashed on a nearby heap of broken flatware.

"A pop instruction," said Mr. Bunny.

"Oh boy!" said the farmer. "Is that how the virtual machine works?"

"That's how this one works," said Mr. Bunny.

Implementation Details

Implementation details are beyond the scope of the Java virtual machine specification. One should not assume that every virtual machine implementation contains a giant squid.

"Show me another trick," said the farmer to the squid, hoping to see some more enchanting sleight of sucker.

Inky was all too happy to oblige. A tentacle quickly wrapped around Farmer Jake's feet and in a flash the old farmer was hanging upside-down. Inky shook several coins out of Farmer Jake's overalls, then plopped him down in the dirt.

The farmer adjusted his hat and watched.

All down his arm Inky's epidermis rippled, and the coins bounced there like jumping beans on a conveyor belt. As each token homed in on its corresponding sucker cup, the squid popped a plate from his tottering operand stack and spun it on a tentacle tip. Suddenly, with a happy clack of his chitinous beak, Inky had those platters spinning on all eight arms at once, and on his two shorter feeding tentacles as well.

What a show!

Farmer Jake clapped enthusiastically.

Then the ground began to move. Farmer Jake and Mr. Bunny and Inky the Squid were being lowered down below the surface on a hydraulic platform!

"Dang," drawled Jake.

"Method call," said Mr. Bunny.

"Just doing my job," said Inky, all the while balancing the spinning plates on his prehensile appendages.

And so down they went, into the heart of the Java Virtual Machine, a trusty rabbit, a crusty farmer, a rusty rake, and a jolly dish-juggling squid in a fishbowl, all carried on a hydraulic lift into the virtual Java underworld.

Inside the Java Virtual Machine

There is much confusion between Inky the runtime interpreter (an implemntation of the virtual machine specification), and the abstract JVM specification itself. The following analogy should serve to add to this confusion.

Just as Inky the squid has many arms, the Java virtual machine has many subsystems. In this dissection we will take a look inside the thick mantle tube of the Java virtual machine.

Orient the Java Virtual Machine so that the ventral end faces toward you, and make an incision from the collar to the dorsal end.

Locate the heap. This is a sac filled with an inky melanin pigment corresponding to an area of memory shared by all executing threads. What do you suppose would happen if the ink sac sprung a leak? What a mess! Java is designed to prevent this.

The method area holds information about loaded classes. To see it, trace the branchial veins of the gills dorsally to where they meet. Membranous tissues bind it to the constant pool. Go ahead, poke it; you will be unable to make any changes.

Next, expose the buccal bulb within the center of the ring of arms and carefully make an incision to expose the class loader subsystem. A squid has a beak, a tongue-like ligula, and a radula consisting of numerous minute teeth. Similarly, the Java class loader subsystem includes a primordial class loader, ClassLoader objects, and name-spaces. Once a class is siphoned in through the mouth area, it is masticated and digested and pumped by the systemic heart to the sponge-like Java stacks.

This should give you more than enough information to ace your next technical interview.

Summary

- Do not go swimming for at least one hour after eating.
- Do not eat until at least one hour after reading this analogy.

Exercises

1. Fill in the _____.
2. I Know What You _____ Last Summer
3. Bo _____ly Beat
4. _____ Pro Quo

Where to Go Next

Calamari anyone?

8

"I never said it."
—Carl Sagan, *Billions and Billions*

Deep Sky API

Object-oriented programming has been around for some time now, and Java gives us a chance to explain it all over again.

The world is full of objects—there are well over seventy of them. And new objects are being discovered all the time, especially if you look under your cushions. Software engineers were quick to embrace objects—at least those that weren't sticky and covered with lint[1]—as an effective means of encapsulation, thus ending the age of free-range data.

And that brings us to our first OO buzzword: *data encapsulation*.

 Data encapsulation refers to the ability of objects to hide their guts from prying eyes (except maybe those of a qualified proctologist).

The original motivation behind data hiding is not well understood, as most of the data on this seminal event have been hidden. But it is likely that programmers were embarrassed by their poor choice of variable names, and wished for a way to conceal them. If the variable names were hidden inside some sort of object—like a shoebox under the bed—nobody would see that you had obsessively used your girlfriend's (or boyfriend's) name as a network packet pointer or global file handle. And if you broke up with your boyfriend (or girlfriend), you would need a way to change the variable name without breaking any dependencies in an extended custody battle.

---

1. The objects, not the engineers.

In a large C project, changing a widely used variable is not unlike having a tattoo removed. C++ tried to solve the problem with the *private* keyword, but it was found that people opened the headers and peeked at the variable names anyway. So Java got rid of the header files. But then it gave savvy snoops a secret map (javap) to those goofy variable names, and now you're back to square one.

 Avoid the use of data. Write pure code.

Meanwhile, back in the real world, most programmers have not freed themselves from the material allure of data, so an object-oriented language must provide some method of manipulating the messy stuff. The method is *methods*.

 Methods get the parentheses.

If variables are nouns, methods are verbs. And comments are adjectives, and parentheses are prepositions, and dangling pointers are like that embarrassing piece of toilet paper stuck to the heel of your shoe, but Java has solved this problem as well (the pointer problem, that is; you're on your own with the toilet paper thing).

The First Object

Objects were among the earliest discoveries of man, right after gossip, nose picking, and monkey impersonations.

One of the first objects was a large smooth rock that belonged to a Neanderthal named Skippy. (Some experts insist the proper name is *Scooter*. Here we use the more widely accepted translation.) Skippy noticed that his rock easily rolled downhill, and he used this discovery to impress his friends with the first patent.[1] And so it is that since the so-called Age of Skippy we have been continually reinventing the ball.

But it took tens of thousands of years to put objects to use in any kind of programming language, largely due to the difficulty of attracting good programmers during the Dark Ages, when it was hard to find a decent 401(k) plan.

---

1. For a moss prevention mechanism.

And so where does this succinct introduction to objects leave us?

In the Dark

"Where are we?" asked Farmer Jake when the hydraulic lift finally came to a halt. "It's so dark." Indeed, in the darkness the old farmer could barely see that funny Mr. Bunny or Inky in his dinky bowl.

"You haven't instantiated any objects yet," said the squid. "There's nothing to see."

"The squid is right," said Mr. Bunny. "In Java, you can't do much without objects. An application without objects is like a protoplanetary disk without clods of chondritic material."

"Then let's make some!" said Jake.

"Not so fast," said Mr. Bunny. "First you need to learn about classes."

"Dang, it's always something," said Farmer Jake.

"Follow me!" said Inky.

Farmer Jake was hoping he wouldn't need to jump into the fishbowl with the squid (he hadn't brought his bathing trunks[1]), so his mind was put at ease when Inky jumped right out of the bowl and hoisted it up onto his back. "Right this way," chirped the squid.

And so Mr. Bunny and Farmer Jake followed Inky as he slimed a glowing trail, water sloshing from the bowl on his back.

The Java API

They entered a thick forest of tree structures and branching code paths. Mr. Bunny and Farmer Jake followed Inky's glowing slime trail through the darkness and around the following sidebar.

Slime Trails

A *slime trail* is a series of stylistically similar hacks in a large software project, often produced by an inept programmer who was later promoted.
Usage: *I followed the slime trail and arrived at the squid.*

Farmer Jake heard the hum of unseen machinery.

"What's that noise?" he asked. "Is it the virtual machine?"

"No," whispered Mr. Bunny. "We discussed the virtual machine in the last chapter. It must be the DMMC."

That acronym again.

As if on cue Farmer Jake heard a distant motorcycle Doppler-shift through several gears. He clutched his rake tighter. Suddenly headlights flashed through the trees, wheels spun on gravel, and he found himself choking on a whirlwind of

---

1. Little did he know that soon enough he would take a swim. See Chapter 10.

dust. Then there was silence and darkness, except for Inky's slime trail glowing on the forest floor.

"Gee, Mr. Bunny, it sure is dark," moaned Farmer Jake. He wished for one of Mr. Bunny's bright little friends—Freddy Flashlight or Tommy Torch or even Glinda the Glow-in-the-Dark Keychain—to shed some light on the situation.

"I'll see what I can do," said Mr. Bunny. He reached into his magic rucksack, and out popped—

—a fistful of yesterday's mashed potatoes.

"Buffer's corrupted again," said Mr. Bunny.

"I thought that couldn't happen in Java," said Jake.

"Bad programming practices can overcome any language," said Mr. Bunny. "It's the DMMC for sure."

They reached an incline and began to climb. Jake huffed and puffed, and Mr. Bunny hopped along beside him. When they emerged above the tree line, the slime trail ended. Inky was gone!

"Look!" said Farmer Jake.

Above them the dome of the sky was alive with blinky twinkly stars. They stood on a hillside. The stars looked close enough to touch.

"Sure are a lot of stars," said Farmer Jake.

"Those are the core Java classes," explained Mr. Bunny.

"Sure are a lot of classes, then," replied the Farmer.

"Billions and billions," winked Mr. Bunny. To Farmer Jake they looked like Plate 1.

Plate 1 *The Java API*

Star Tour

The many classes that comprise the Java API can indeed be overwhelming. Let's spread a blanket on the hillside and listen in as Mr. Bunny gives Farmer Jake a stargazer's tour of the API.

"Look," said Mr. Bunny. "There's the `BigDecimal`." Mr. Bunny pointed to a decimal-shaped asterism in the night sky.

Asterism 1 *The BigDecimal*

"And if you follow the stars to the north, they lead to the `Object` class...there!"

Farmer Jake followed the pointer stars of the `BigDecimal`—even though there are no pointers in Java—and saw the star Mr. Bunny was talking about.

"What's so special about the `Object` class?" asked Farmer Jake.

"The `Object` class is the North Star of the Java class hierarchy," said Mr. Bunny. "All the other classes revolve around it. If you can find the `Object` class, you can trace a path to all the constellations in the sky. For example, if you look this way"—he pointed to the west—"you'll see the AWT classes."

Farmer Jake tried to see the shape that Mr. Bunny was talking about, but there were just too many stars. So Mr. Bunny took a marker from his pocket protector and hopped up onto Farmer Jake's shoulders.

The stars really *were* close enough to touch!

Mr. Bunny traced the outline of the AWT classes with the marker, drawing right on the sky, as shown in Chart 1.

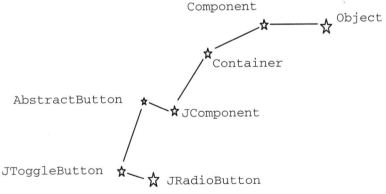

Chart 1 *Abstract Windows Toolkit*

"And over here is the `String` class," said the bunny rabbit. Farmer Jake leaned to the south so Mr. Bunny could trace the constellation outline. See Map 1.

Map 1 *Stringus Major*

"What's that one?" asked Farmer Jake, pointing to another part of the sky. "That's the LinkageError class," said Mr. Bunny.

Farmer Jake used his imagination, and thought he could make out a linkage error in the cluster of stars.

Some Visible Classes

Standing on Farmer Jake's shoulders, Mr. Bunny sketched the outlines of the other Java core classes. The classes you will be able to see depend on your latitude, time of year, and JDK version. Some are described below.

Class	Description
AdjustmentEvent	Event fired by Orion's belt after a big meal.
ContainerEvent	A Tupperware party.
DataFlavor	33rd most popular at Baskin Robbins.
PipedWriter	Samuel Taylor Coleridge.
PixelGrabber	Deprecated pending resolution of the sexual harassment suit.
PlainView	Where to hide.
Scrollbar	Hangout for archaeologists.
SecurityManager	Derived from PoliceAcademyDropout.
System	Provides system-independent access to system resources through a system-independent API. **Note:** In many cases the system-independent API is not system independent and should not be used.
ZipOutputStream	Local ordinances may prohibit public use of this class.
	The Crab Nebula.

Instantiating Objects

Finally Mr. Bunny hopped down from Farmer Jake's shoulders. He had diagramed all of the constellations! Farmer Jake even saw his Zodiac sign (Leo the `LinkedList`).

"How can I instantiate one o' them classes?" asked the farmer.

Just then a shooting star passed overhead.

"Make a wish," said Mr. Bunny.

So Farmer Jake made a wish.

```
String s = new String;
```

Suddenly a `String` object was wiggling on the ground in front of Farmer Jake. The old geezer giggled with glee. When another falling star passed overhead, Farmer Jake made another wish. A `ListUI` zoomed out of the sky.

Soon the landscape was lit by a spectacular meteor shower as Farmer Jake wished for more and more objects. "Yummy," said the farmer as he bit into a buttery `BeanDescriptor`. "Some of these classes are tasty."

"Just don't wish for a `VirtualMachineError`," cautioned Mr. Bunny. But Farmer Jake wasn't listening. He wished for a `Button`, `Box`, and `Boolean`, and a calendar by Julian.[1] Then things got really scary when a rhyming `Dictionary` fluttered down. A `Byte` and `Float` and `Long` and `Double` fell out of the sky in a pile of rubble. Farmer Jake rubbed his bristly stubble. His programming style was nothing but trouble!

That hillside was getting crowded.

He stuck a `Socket` in his pocket as he scrimmaged with an `Image`. He was heckled by `Vector` and a prying `Introspector`, caught a `FileNotFoundException`, dropped a `URLConnection`, and it changed his whole complexion when a `PhantomReference` hexed him in a ball of `Thread` and `String`—what a tangle of a thing!—with a capital T and that rhymes with P and that stands for `ProgressMonitorInputStream`.

"What should I do?" cried Farmer Jake.

"Well," said Mr. Bunny thoughtfully as the confusion mounted around him. "You should probably instantiate an `Applet` object. That might let us do something useful."

Creating Subclasses

Many of the classes in the Java API are designed to serve as subsets (or superclasses) for subclasses (or supersets) that you define. The terminology can be

---

1. Not all wishes come true. Java 1.1 supports only the GregorianCalendar class.

quite confusing, but once you master it, you'll be able to baffle even yourself.

 A *subclass* is a *superset* of a *superclass* and a *superclass* is a *subset* of its *subclass*.

"In order to do anything useful with the `Applet` class, one must derive a subclass," explained Mr. Bunny.

To define a subclass in Java, use the following syntax:

```
class Subclass extends Object {
private:
    Boolean periscopeUp = FALSE;
public:
    Subclass() {;}
    void upPeriscope() {periscopeUp = True;}
}
```

To get this to compile in C, a few simple changes are required:

```
/* class Subclass extends Object { */
/* private: */
/* Boolean periscopeUp = FALSE; */
/* public: */
/* Subclass() {;} */
/* void upPeriscope() {periscopeUp = True;} */
/* } */
```

MyApplet the Horse

The hillside was crowded with the objects Farmer Jake had created. They nipped at his ankles and snaked up his overalls.

Farmer Jake had listened very patiently while Mr. Bunny explained about subclasses and superclasses, but—OUCH! A `Byte` nibbled a bit out of his shin—it was time to get out of there!

So Farmer Jake looked up at the `Applet` class in the sky and made a very special kind of wish.

```
public class MyApplet extends Applet
```

A great winged horse appeared.

"Oh boy, what a nice horsey!" he said.

"Hop on," cried Mr. Bunny as a `BevelBorder` bounced a `Book` off a `BufferedWriter`'s bean. The objects were out of control!

Farmer Jake hopped onto his applet, `MyApplet`, and Mr. Bunny climbed up behind him.

"Giddyap!" cried Mr. Bunny, invoking the `start()` method.

And with a start, `MyApplet` started.

Summary

In the Java API there are billions and billions *TO BE CONTINUED IN THE NEXT REVISION*

Exercises

1. Connect the dots:

Where to Go Next

Let's get Sirius.

9

'Tis in my memory lock'd,
And you yourself shall keep the key of it.
—William Shakespeare
Java How to Program

Square Bracket Bric-a-brac

Mr. Bunny and Farmer Jake rode MyApplet the Horse into the predawn light, leaving all of Farmer Jake's objects behind. As the stars faded from view, Farmer Jake made a mental note to purchase some documentation of the Java API.

A ray of light reached over the horizon, followed by another and another—and another—and another—until an array of rays had raided the sky and stolen the last star like a pickpocket lifting code from an online sample. Then Mr. Sunrise stepped aside and Mr. Sun himself vaulted over the hills and smiled down as if to say "Howdy, Mr. Bunny," but the fiery orb was of course more than ninety-two million miles away and quite impossible to hear across the pitiless, lifeless void of depthless deep black space.

A new day had begun!

Introduction to Arrays

"You can use a variable to hold a reference to a single instance of a class," said Mr. Bunny. "But if you want to code with the big kids, you must use *arrays*."

"I'm thirsty," said Farmer Jake.

"This is very dry material," agreed Mr. Bunny.

Farmer Jake spotted a memory pool in the distance. An unusual pair of monuments towered over it.

"Look, there's Stonehenge," said Farmer Jake.

Mr. Bunny gave his farmer friend a Druidic stare. "Those are the subscripting brackets used for array notation," said the little bunny. See Lesson 1.

Lesson 1 *Stonehenge*

"And on the winter solstice, the rays of the setting sun pass precisely between them," the rabbit added with a wink.

Farmer Jake licked his parched lips and headed for the memory pool under the array subscripting brackets.

What Is an Array?[1]

An array [2] is a number [2] of subscripting brackets [ ] containing a number of variables indexed by a number or variable or expression.

To declare an array, just drop a pair of square brackets into your code. For consistency, you are allowed to put the brackets before or after the variable name.

The brackets can be imported from an old C program that you don't need anymore.

The following examples show how to declare a ten [10] element array:

Example [1]:
```
short[] example = new short[10];
```

Example [2]:
```
short example[] = new short[10];
```

Wrong:
```
short example[] = new short[11];
```

Example [1] creates an array called `example`. In the example [2] example `example[]` is also an array called `example`.

Array subscripts [3] always start at zero [0],[3][4], therefore `example[1]` is the second [2nd] element of `example[]`, and it follows that the previous [1st] element is accessed by `example[0]`.[4]. To avoid confusion, the first [1st] element [0] of an array is called the 0th element to distinguish it from the second [2nd][1] element and prevent an off-by-one [1] error.[5]

Off by What?

The so-called "off by one" error is so common that the mistake itself may one day be voted on by a standards committee, and will thereafter be a required error. But expect this action to be deferred until after eradication of the famous "off by 100" millennium bug.

Bounds Checking

Sooner or later even the best little bunny is bound to bound beyond the bounds of an array. If you attempt to access an out of bounds array element (such as `example[10]`in the ten [10] element array `example[]` of examples [1] and [2]), the `ArrayIndexOutOfBoundsException[6][7][8][9][10]`[1] is thrown.

Double-Subscripted Arrays

To create a double-subscripted array [11][12] just add more brackets as in example [3].

Example [3]:
```
short my_array[][] = new short[11][12];
```
It is possible to leave out the last dimension (e.g. [12] of [11][12] of example [3]) of a double-subscripted array, deferring the creation of each row until you can look up the references [13] at the end of this chapter [9] and figure out how.

---

1. Do not confuse the `ArrayIndexOutOfBoundsException` exception with the `NameOfExceptionIsWayTooLongException` exception.

A Sip from the Memory Pool

Now Farmer Jake was really thirsty. All those bracket references and reference brackets had baked his brain and parched his throat, so he creaked down onto his knees for a sip of water from the pool.

"Yuck," he said, spitting it out.

The water, of course, was brackish.

Summary

[1][2][3][4][5][6][7][8][9][10][11][12][13][14]

References[14]

1. Laurence,Vanhelsuwé. Phillips, Ivan. Hsu, Goang-Tay. Shankar, Krishna. Ries, Eric. Rohaly, Tim. Zukowski, John. "Mastering Java™," p. 170
2. Chan, Patrick. "The Java™ Developer's Almanac," p. 170
3. Deitel, H.M., Deitel, P.J. "Java How to Program," p. 230
4. Gosling, James. Joy, Bill. Steele, Guy. "The Java™ Language Specification," p. 195
5. Deitel, H.M., Deitel, P.J. "Java™ How to Program," p. 232
6. Horstman, Cay S. Cornell, Gary. "Core Java™ Volume I - Fundamentals," p. 576
7. Lindholm, Tim. Yellin, Frank. "The Java™ Virtual Machine Specification," p. 435
8. Kanerva, Jonni. "The Java™ FAQ," p. 69
9. Sowizral, Henry. Rushforth, Kevin. "The Java™ 3D API Specification," p. 425
10. Davis, Stephen R. "Learn Java Now," p. 149.
11. Kernighan, Brian W. Ritchie, Dennis M. "The C Programming Language, Second Edition," p. 110.
12. Rinehart, Martin. "Java Programming with Visual J++," p. 32.
13. III, Carlton Egremont. "Mr. Bunny's Big Cup o' Java," p. 74
14. Folks, A Bunch of. "Webster's New Universal Unabridged Dictionary," p. 1206.
15. In the next chapter we'll swim with the fishes and meet the Mayor of Interfaces.

Where to Go Next

[15]

$$\left[10\right]$$

"Ah, Juicy Fruit."

—Ken Kesey, *One Flew Over the Cuckoo's Nest*

The Mayor of Interfaces

Mr. Bunny and Farmer Jake rode into a haunting landscape of fumaroles and mud volcanoes and geysers. Farmer Jake nearly gagged on the sulfurous smell of legacy code.

"What is this place?" he asked.

"It's the Java Native Interface," whispered Mr. Bunny.

Their trusty steed, MyApplet, was spooked by the choking fumes and parched earth beneath his feet. Mr. Bunny and Farmer Jake had to dismount and carefully lead MyApplet through the uncommented landscape.

JNI

The Java Native Interface (JNI) allows Java methods to call native methods and native methods to call Java methods and Java methods called by native methods to call native methods and native methods called by Java methods called by native methods to call Java methods and (at the risk of insulting your intelligence) Java methods called by native methods called by Java methods called by native methods called by Java methods called by native methods called by Java methods to call native methods. And so on.

 A *native method* is Java's wrapper for code written in another language. Compare this to Snoop Doggy Dog, a rapper with lyrics written in another language.

JNI allows Java code to invoke methods written in another language such as C or C++. Depiction 1 shows the plumbing at work.

75

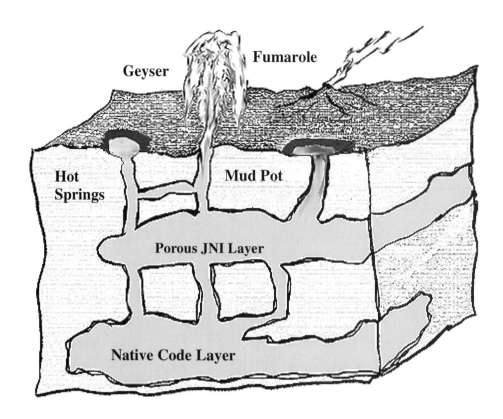

Depiction 1 *The Java Native Interface*

The Logic Dolphin

Mr. Bunny and Farmer Jake stepped carefully around a bubbling mud pot. Just then something crawled out of Farmer Jake's pant leg and slithered across the ground. A `String`! (See Chapter 8.)

MyApplet the Horse whinnied and reared up on his hind data members. Farmer Jake jumped back in surprise—and the fragile ground cracked beneath his feet.

He was sucked into a murky mud pot.

Sanka!

He felt the horse's reins slip from his fingers as he sank below the surface. "Mr. Bunny," he gurgled, but all that came out was the sound of a submerged farmer trying to talk to a rabbit.

Farmer Jake did what he always did when he fell into a mud pot: he hung on to his rake and tried to figure out which way was up. When he thought he had it all worked out, he kicked his legs. But his legs were caught in a tangle of weeds! He flailed about with his rake, but the more he struggled, the tighter the weeds seemed to ensnare him.

It was not unlike an all night debug session.

If only Mr. Bunny were here to save my bacon, thought Farmer Jake. But it was too late; a strip of soggy bacon floated out of his pocket and was gobbled up by minnows.

Farmer Jake felt a funky sinking feeling as he sank into the Sanka. He envisioned spelunking engineers of the future dunking into this sunken world and marvelling at the fossilized remains of a farmer and his well-preserved rake.

Then his flailing arm struck something solid, and his hand gripped a bristly surface. He hung on. Something was pulling him from the weeds!

He gripped tighter, and found himself suddenly free, towed beside a magnificent blue dolphin.

Illustration: Jake swimming with dolphin

Drawing 1 *Farmer Jake and the Logic Dolphin*

Farmer Jake could telepathically feel the dolphin's thoughts.

"Welcome," clicked a dolphin voice inside Farmer Jake's head. "You were caught in a brain marsh."

"A brain marsh?" gurgled the farmer, forgetting he was still submerged.

"Indeed. Obfuscated code is fertile ground for weeds. Haven't you heard of the K.I.S.S. principle?"

"Keep It Simple, Stupid?" Farmer Jake beamed his thoughts through the tines of his rake, which served as an antenna. A bit of a hack, but it worked.

"Kelp Is Seaweed, Silly," replied the dolphin. "Allow me to introduce myself. I am a Logic Dolphin, one of an ancient species that has evolved to abhor sloppy code, rescue lost engineers (although we don't get many farmers), and avoid commercial tuna nets. Because your QWERTY keyboard is non-optimal— and in any case we have no hands—ours is a culture of pure logic."

Spock with flippers, thought Farmer Jake.

"A logical comparison, but we are a far more playful species," said the dolphin, hearing Jake's thoughts. The farmer had neglected to mute his rake.

"Dang," Jake telepathicalized. "So where are you taking me?"

"We logic dolphins always travel the shortest path from point A to point B. I assume that's where you want to go?"

Farmer Jake nodded. He was anxious to get to the point, whatever it might be labelled. So he held on tight while the Logic Dolphin enumerated many common programming errors.

Common Programming Errors

- Dividing by infinity.
- Mistaking the assignment operator for your project leader.
- Discussing politics, religion, or favorite development tools.
- Omitting the .java extension from your résumé.
- Calling no argument constructor when there is no no-argument constructor, a no-no resulting in an argument with the compiler.
- Failure to check result codes, catch exceptions, or negotiate an aggressive stock option vesting schedule.
- Use of runtime type checking without a doctor's prescription.
- Attempting to learn a programming language from a rabbit.
- C.

"Will it ever get better?" gurgled Farmer Jake.

"Don't hold your breath."

Point B

Farmer Jake and the Logic Dolphin skirted a coral reef and passed over another menacing marsh.

"Here's where you get off," said the dolphin at last.

A big fat pipe stuck out of a wall of mud. Jake had enjoyed the dolphin's company, but was beginning to think it would be nice to breathe again. He beamed a telepathic goodbye through his rake as the Logic Dolphin set off on the shortest path to somewhere else.

Then Farmer Jake swam toward the pipe. By the time he heard the giant sucking sound, it was too late.

Old Faithful

Mr. Bunny produced a gold pocket watch, a gift from his late uncle. He watched the second hand and waited patiently. Soon the ground began to vibrate under Mr. Bunny's feet. The vibration turned into a WOBBLE, and the WOBBLE turned into a RUMBLE and the RUMBLE turned into a rush of water as— WOOOSH! a geyser erupted.

And who do you suppose rode the column of water into the air and splashed down next to Mr. Bunny?

Why, it was Farmer Jake!

"Wow!" said Farmer Jake, wringing out his overalls. "You'll never guess where I've been."

He retrieved his rake, but his hat still danced a jig atop the spurting geyser.

"Did you meet any Logic Dolphins?" winked Mr. Bunny.

Interfaces

Interfaces are Java's answer to multiple inheritance. So what is the question of multiple inheritance? Simply this: Why, why, why, OH GOD, WHY?

In C++, if you wish a class to support multiple behaviors, you generally must derive from two or more direct superclasses. Let's start with a simple class called `JavaDude`:

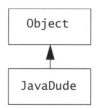

Blueprint 1 *Simple Inheritance*

As shown in Blueprint 1, `JavaDude` lives in a cubicle and knows the way to the supply cabinet.

This is how the class might be defined:

Ja·va·Dude (*jä·va·do͞od*), n. **1.** A contrived class in the book *Mr. Bunny's Big Cup o' Java*.

Now suppose we want to teach `JavaDude` some new tricks, such as how to walk and chew gum. We could simply add a `chew()` and `walk()` method directly to JavaDude, but then this example would be over. No, we must find a way to make this more complicated.

In C++, we could encapsulate chewing in a Chewy class, and walking in a Walker class, then adjust the antenna in JavaDude's living room, as shown in Sketch 1.

Sketch 1 *Multiple Inheritance*

This is known as *multiple inheritance*. Think of multiple inheritance as the rabbit-ear antenna of programming.

In Java, the same thing can be accomplished by subscribing to cable.

Interface This

A Java *interface* defines a set of methods that don't exist. Because the methods don't exist, you get to implement them yourself in any way you see fit, so long as their antics conform to the semantics.

By defining methods that don't exist, you create a powerful polymorphic prenuptial agreement whereby users of the interface defer marriage until runtime.[1]

Interfaces are defined by writing some code. The Chewy interface might be coded as follows:

```
bloobie doobie snoobie floopie floo
{
    ker-WEEEE!
},
```

but only if you are a blithering idiot.

A somewhat less idiotic way to define the Chewy interface is shown below:

```
interface Chewy
{
    double m(int gum);
}
```

This at least will compile, and (if I have correctly decoded subliminal messages received via television) it will help you meet twins.

Now let's define the Walker interface:

```
interface Walker
{
    long walk(short pier);
}
```

Reach out with your feelings, Luke.

Putting together all we have learned, we can implement the Chewy and Walker interfaces as shown in Listing 1.

Listing 1

---

1. In other words, you should read another book if you really want to figure this out.

Window 1 shows the applet running in a browser.

Window 1 *Front View*

The Mayor of Interfaces

"Dang!" said Farmer Jake. "I hope I didn't leave the iron on."

The farmer and the rabbit had arrived in a small dusty town. They rode MyApplet down `main()` street and dismounted near a coffee shop. Inside, a painter was scraping old lettering from the window. Farmer Jake could still make out the name:

BLEEKER'S
CAFE

Side View

The rich smell of coffee mingled with the ripe odor of fermenting garbage as a sanitation truck pulled up to the curb where Farmer Jake was scraping gum from the bottom of his shoe.

"Mornin'," said Jake to the truck driver.

The driver scowled. "Some darn fool left a bunch of unreferenced objects up on Derby Dingle," he grumbled. Sure enough, the back of the truck was full of all the objects Farmer Jake had instantiated on the hillside in Chapter 8.

Farmer Jake averted his eyes and tugged down his hat brim and continued scraping his shoe.

Garbage Collection

Most Java Virtual Machine implementations use some form of garbage collection to recycle memory, transforming the morning's burnt waffles into a brand new BMW, or stitching an Armani suit from your moldy melon rinds.

Unfortunately, automatic garbage collection is not available for all those unused AOL disks.

Mr. Bunny and Farmer Jake tied MyApplet the Horse to a nearby traffic light and stepped inside the coffee shop.

It was empty, except for the painter. "Just a minute, fellas," he said. He had sketched in the outline of a new name. Farmer Jake watched as the painter dabbed his brush in the GUI paint and filled in the new lettering.

"Under new management," explained the painter, rinsing his brush. Then he turned and RRIIIPPPP!—stripped off his coveralls. They had been held together with Velcro. Underneath he wore a sheriff's uniform.

"Gee, I thought he was a painter," whispered Farmer Jake.

"Watch carefully," said Mr. Bunny. "This fellow implements multiple interfaces."

"Hold it right there!" said the sheriff, placing a Velcro badge on his chest. "I told you boys if you stuck your nose back in this county, you'd never see daylight again as long as you live."

"I'm Mr. Bunny," said the perky rabbit. "And this is my friend Farmer Jake." Jake tipped his hat with his rake.

"You just hop back on yer motorbikes and git!" snapped the sheriff.

"But we came on a horse," said Farmer Jake.

"No motorcycles?" asked the sheriff.

Farmer Jake checked his pockets and shrugged.

"Well then, I guess you're okay."

The sheriff stepped behind the counter. RRIIIPPPP! Off came the sheriff's uniform. He was a bartender! "What'll it be, boys?"

"Two big cups o' java!" said Mr. Bunny.

The painter-sheriff-bartender set two steaming cups of coffee down on the bar, then tore at his clothes one more time.

RRIIIPPPP!

Farmer Jake covered his eyes. "Is he in his skivvies?"

No, the bartender wore a tuxedo. He adjusted his bowtie and puffed himself up and shook Mr. Bunny's paw. "I hope I can count on your support!" he said in a big mayoral voice. He turned to Farmer Jake. "Vote Interfaces!"

A beefy hand squeezed pain down Farmer Jake's repetitive-stress-injured hand. "You must be the Mayor of Interfaces!" said the farmer.

"Well, I'm not the Viceroy of Velcro!" laughed the Mayor. "Would you care to make an illegal campaign contribution?"

"Now do you understand interfaces?" asked Mr. Bunny. "By hiding the implementation details, you ensure you never get caught."

Farmer Jake nodded, massaging his cramped mouse finger.

Just then the roar of forty modified mufflers filled the air.

"They're back," said the Mayor, suddenly frightened.

"Who's back?" asked the farmer.

"The DMMC."

Mr. Bunny and Farmer Jake and the Mayor of Interfaces went through the door of the café and stepped outside.

The Deprecated Method Motorcycle Club was drag-racing in the street.

Summary

This chapter taught you the basic hydrology of the Java Native Interface, and digressed into something about a dolphin. Then you learned about another kind of interface, the *interface*, which was represented by some guy who kept changing his clothes.

Exercises

1. Identify the following.

    A.   B.   C.   D.

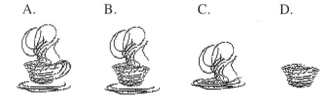

2. Unscramble the secret message:

    ```
    bloobie doobie snoobie floopie floo ker-WEEEE
    ```

3. Make sure you've turned off the iron.

Where to Go Next

In the next chapter we will do some multithreaded programming and finally learn more about the DMMC. We will also improve our chewing and walking technique.

"We're gonna wait for Crazy."
—*The Wild One*

Thread Time

In this chapter we build on our `JavaDude` example. (Well actually, we're going to throw all our work away and start over.)

As you recall from the previous chapter, our `JavaDude` class learned how to walk and chew gum by implementing the `Chewy` and `Walker` interfaces. In this chapter, we will teach `JavaDude` how to walk and chew gum at the same time.

To accomplish this, we will use a technique called *tricky programming*. Get out your sewing kit, kiddies. It's time to play with threads.

 A *thread* is a single sequential flow of control within a program or argyle sock.

Threads let more than one thing happen at once inside your program. All programs start out with a single thread of execution. Many programs stay single, and never know the pitter-patter of little feet.

So let's give `JavaDude` some cool threads.

The `Thread` class is the base class for threads. It has an empty `run()` method. By implementing your own `run()` method, you can make a thread that chews when it runs:

```
class ChewThread extends Thread  // class ChewThread extends Thread
{
    public void run()// public void run()
    {  // for i equals zero, i less than ten, i plus plus
       for (int i = 0; i<10; i++)
```

```
      {
          System.out.println("chomp"); // Sys-
tem.out.println("chomp")
      }
   }
}
```

Next, we write a class that walks when it runs:

```
class WalkThread extends Thread
{ // open curly brace
   public void run()
   { // open curly brace
      for (int i = 0; i<10; i++)
      { // open curly brace
         if (i%2 == 0)
            { // open curly brace
               System.out.println("left"); // no comment
            } // close curly brace
         else
            { // open curly brace
               System.out.println("right");
            } // close curly brace
      } // close curly brace
   } // close curly brace
} // close curly brace
```

Except for the differences, this class is exactly the same as the ChewThread class.

Now all we need to do to make our JavaDude walk and chew gum at the same time is create an instance of the WalkThread and ChewThread classes and start them up.

```
public class JavaDude extends Object
{ // comments omitted for clarity
   public static void main(String args[])
   {
      new WalkThread().start();
      new ChewThread().start();
   }
}
```

Because the threads run asynchronously, the output will vary slightly each time JavaDude takes a walk. The output might look like this:

```
left
right
chomp
```

```
left
chomp
right
chomp
left
chomp
right
chomp
left
chomp
right
chomp
left
chomp
right
chomp
chomp
```

Or this:

```
left
right
chomp
left
right
left
chomp
right
left
right
left
chomp
right
chomp
chomp
chomp
chomp
chomp
chomp
chomp
```

Or this:

```
left
chomp
right
chomp
left
chomp
right
chomp
```

```
left
chomp
right
chomp
left
chomp
right
chomp
left
chomp
right
chomp
```

Or this:
```
left
chomp
right
left
chomp
right
chomp
left
right
left
right
left
chomp
chomp
chomp
chomp
chomp
chomp
right
chomp
```

Or this:
```
left
chomp
right
chomp
left
right
left
chomp
right
chomp
left
chomp
right
```

```
chomp
left
chomp
chomp
chomp
right
chomp
```

Or this:

```
left
right
chomp
left
chomp
right
chomp
left
chomp
right
chomp
left
chomp
right
chomp
left
chomp
right
chomp
chomp[1]
```

Note how the walking and chewing are intermingled. JavaDude takes a few steps, then chomps his gum. Then he takes a few more steps, and chomps and chomps, and steps, and chomps, and steps, lurching down the corridor, bumping into people, knocking things over, desperate for a soda.

He's uncoordinated, but what a programmer!

Thread Priority

Java supports a deterministic scheduling algorithm called *change the priority and see if it makes any difference*. The Thread class lets you set the priority of a thread by using the setPriority method.

To set a thread's priority pick a number between one (MIN_PRIORITY) and ten (MAX_PRIORITY) and pass it to setPriority. The value is immediately transmitted to a secret government agency (the same one that has been suppressing the

---

1. Oops, this one's the same as the first example. Sorry to be so repetitive.

cheese doodle), where it is combined with the number of times you press that use-less elevator Close Door button and plotted against the setting of the darkness control on your toaster oven.

The resulting curve has nothing to do with your thread's priority, but is known to correlate well with long-term stock market trends.

Wild Ones

The motorcycles roared through the sleepy town. The sleepy town rolled over and yawned and punched the snooze alarm, but to no avail. Bikers in black leather jackets and white T-shirts and skin-tight jeans tossed beer bottles into the street, threatening havoc and last minute design changes.

"Who are they?" blinked Farmer Jake.

"The DMMC," said the Mayor of Interfaces.

"Deprecated methods," said Mr. Bunny. "Outcasts."

"They run in a different thread than the rest of us," said the Mayor.

Farmer Jake turned at the sound of drunken laughter. Bikers were emptying trash cans onto the sidewalk. The garbage collector was trying desperately to con-trol the situation, but everywhere were greasy grimy gopher guts and roly poly fish heads and videotapes of the Howard Stern show. Farmer Jake was disgusted, but he couldn't look away.

"I wish they'd grow up," said a woman's voice. It was a waitress walking toward them with a bag of groceries. "They're just boys, you know. Especially Johnny."

At the mention of Johnny's name, a motorcycle roared by in a haze of blue smoke. The waitress's grocery bag ripped and sand poured out of the bottom.

"Show off," she said. "He's corrupted my data."

Farmer Jake looked pleadingly at Mr. Bunny, but the rabbit had his own prob-lems. Mr. Bunny reached into his rucksack—and out popped a pile of biodegrad-able packing peanuts.

Thread Synchronization

Earlier in this chapter you saw `JavaDude`'s asynchronous lurching chomping gait, the result of the somewhat random system-dependent scheduling of his chewing and walking threads. But did you get a good look at the clothes he was wearing? Sheesh!

 Don't wear stripes with plaid.

The *synchronized* keyword protects a method from concurrent threads. Perhaps this is information Mr. Bunny could use.

Synchronized Bikers

The gang was back in a race condition, zooming up and down the main street of the town, terrorizing the residents. Farmer Jake held onto his hat as a biker zoomed by and almost knocked him over.

"Mr. Bunny, do something!"

But Mr. Bunny had already done something. "Step inside the circle!" he cried.

Mr. Bunny had traced a circle in the dirt outside the café. Farmer Jake and the Mayor of Interfaces and the waitress with the bag of sand stepped inside the circumference with the clever rabbit.

A motorcycle raced down the street and skidded to a stop inside the circle. It was getting crowded!

"Johnny!" scolded the waitress.

"Man, you are too square," said Johnny, revving his motorcycle defiantly.

Another biker buzzed them, but stopped short of entering. As long as one motorcycle was inside, no others could penetrate. Mr. Bunny had cleverly formed a synchronized circle of protection around his friends!

The cycle gang circled the circle, engines revving hot in the afternoon sun. Around and around they went, ready and waiting, but unable to run, as shown in Cycle 1.

The waitress continued to scold Johnny.

"Why don't you all just go on a picnic, instead of bothering these good folks with your data-corrupting ways," she suggested.

"That's cornball style," scoffed Johnny. "We gotta wail, put down some jive. You dig, daddy-o?"

"What are you rebelling against?" asked Farmer Jake.

"What have you got?" replied Johnny.

Farmer Jake shrugged. "Got me some chickens," he said. "And a lettuce patch."

"He won't listen to reason," said the Mayor. "He and his gang member methods were deprecated back in 1.0, and they've been terrorizing the town ever since."

"That's right, man," said Johnny. "You folks act like you're too good for me. Somebody acts like that, I knock 'em around, and...hey, nice rake!"

Johnny was struck with sudden admiration.

Farmer Jake tightened his grip on the rake's well-worn handle.

"Would you like it?" asked Mr. Bunny, who up to now had been busy rebooting his corrupted rucksack.

"Do you mean it?" asked Johnny. "You'd give a rake like that to a trouble-maker like me?"

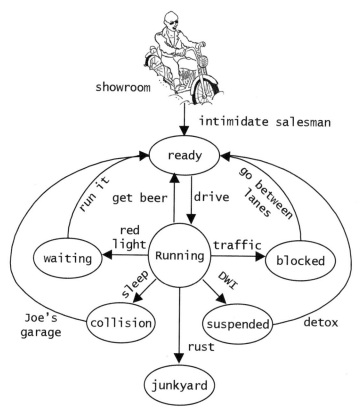

Cycle 1 *When Threads Go Bad*

"Mr. Bunny," moaned Farmer Jake. "It's my favorite!"

"Well," said Mr. Bunny, "I don't see any other way out. Do you, Johnny?"

Johnny shuffled his feet nervously. He sure wanted that rake!

"Johnny, you and your deprecated gang feel like outcasts because...well, because you are," said Mr. Bunny. "But you're just as good as everyone else. The only thing the others have that you don't..."

"Is a place in the documentation?" interrupted Johnny.

"I was thinking of something like this!" Mr. Bunny reached into his reinitialized rucksack—and out popped the biggest racing trophy Johnny had ever seen!

"Wow, man," said Johnny, taking the trophy. "You're really hip to my jive. Let's go, boys! Last one to Palo Alto buys the beers!"

And with the trophy perched on his handlebars, Johnny the outlaw leader of the DMMC sped off to find new towns to terrorize, his gang following behind.

"I wonder if he'll ever get to Redmond," said the waitress wistfully.

Mr. Bunny just wiggled his ears and zipped up his rucksack.

Summary

A multithreaded program can have several threads of execution all running at the same time, thrashing it out over who gets to use the shared resources. It all ends with a chase scene and somebody getting killed.

Exercises

1. Identify the following:

**(String s);**

Where to Go Next

Home, James.

"There's no place like [Farmer Jake's kitchen]."
—Dorothy

Home Sweet Home Page

Well, together we have been on a journey of non-stop learning.[1] Let's lighten up, take a big breath, and review.

First we learned that Java is a programming language. (If you bought this book hoping for a career in refrigeration, you probably put it down several chapters ago. Which is a shame because you've just missed the only *freon* reference.)

Next we visited some Java primitives and almost caused an international incident. Fortunately the Java primitive data types have consistent sizes across platforms, so such incidents can generally be avoided.

When writing cross-platform code, be sure to leave Farmer Jake at home.

We then met Foxy and Telly and Inky and the Mayor of Interfaces and the deprecated methods' rebellious leader, Johnny. So now you are ready for a lucrative career as a Java programmer. Although the highest paying jobs require at least 15 years of Java programming experience, the hours you've spent studying this book have certainly helped to waste some of that time.

And though there's nothing left to learn, there's still more time to waste.

---

1. Yeah, right.

The Proclamation

The whole town had gathered to thank Mr. Bunny for running off the gang of deprecated methods. Farmer Jake was especially grateful because he still had his favorite garden rake.

The Mayor of Interfaces came out of the café to make a speech. He carried a bulky briefcase and looked quite important in his painter's cap and black tuxedo, with a sheriff badge Velcroed to his chest and a beer-soaked bar rag for a boutonniere.

"A proclamation!" he proclaimed.

The crowd applauded.

The Mayor of Interfaces made a big deal out of opening his briefcase. It contained a folding stool which he stood on the sidewalk. Then he closed the briefcase and placed it on the stool, and made no further reference to it.

The printed proclamation he pulled from his shirt. And read.

"Whereas our town has been terrorized by deprecated methods ever since version 1.0...

"And whereas we didn't know what to do about it other than encouraging everyone to ignore them....

"And whereas Mr. Bunny came to town and gave them a racing trophy...

"And whereas apparently this is all they ever wanted, which will never make a damn bit of sense to me, but what the heck....

"I now proclaim this to be Mr. Bunny Day!"

The crowd cheered.

"HOORAY!"

Then hushed.

Mr. Bunny bowed to the Mayor. Then the furry little fellow turned to address the townsfolk. A gentle breeze teased the rabbit's ears.

The garbage collector swept away the Mayor's unreferenced briefcase.

Somewhere a bird chirped.

"Java is good," said Mr. Bunny.

The crowd nodded.

The Leap Home

It was time for Mr. Bunny and Farmer Jake to go home. They had come to a virtual land far from the physical world we know, and yet, as you have seen, not so very different.

"What should we do," moaned Farmer Jake. "Bessie will be gettin' worried."

"I can offer you a ride in my limo," said the Mayor of Interfaces. "But only to the edge of town."

"It's a start!" said Mr. Bunny.

So Mr. Bunny and Farmer Jake hopped into the back of the limo, and with the rip of a Velcro strip or two, the Mayor implemented a driver interface and climbed behind the wheel.

The back of the limo smelled like chlorine. There was a swimming pool back there! The water sloshed as the limo lurched forward.

"Go ahead, soak your tired feet," said the driver.

Farmer Jake hesitated. Something was in the water. A fin!

"Mr. Bunny, look!" cried the farmer.

But Mr. Bunny was busy suiting up in his cute little bunny scuba gear.

"Better put this on," said Mr. Bunny, reaching into his rucksack and pulling out a face mask and tank and regulator for Farmer Jake.

Farmer Jake struggled to put the rig on.

"Driver, we won't need to go much further," said Mr. Bunny. "We've found our way home."

And just then the surface of the water rippled and broke, and a dolphin stood up on his tail.

A Logic Dolphin!

"Howdy, Mr. Bunny," clicked the dolphin.

"Let's go!" said Mr. Bunny.

"Mmff," said Farmer Jake through his face mask.

And the rabbit and the farmer splashed into the pool with the Logic Dolphin—and were gone.

Meanwhile, Back at the Ranch

Bessie was puttering around the house. "Dang that old coot," she said. "He's got chores to do before the sun goes down."

Then she heard a commotion in Farmer Jake's cup of coffee, still on the table from breakfast.

Just Ducky

"Where are we?" said Farmer Jake.

The Logic Dolphin had led them safely through a series of nasty brain marshes. They surfaced in what looked like another mud pot, but this one had tall smooth sides, impossible to climb.

They sure couldn't just bob there in the muddy goo, so Mr. Bunny reached into his rucksack— and out popped Ducky Tub Toy!

"How are you doing?" said Ducky.

"Ducky," said Mr. Bunny.

Ducky had been cramped in the crowded rucksack, but now his life-raft-like body could begin to inflate.

And inflate it did. Mr. Bunny and Farmer Jake jumped onto Ducky's back as he inflated.

And Ducky kept on inflating.

And so did Mr. Bunny and Farmer Jake!

"Look, everything's getting smaller!" said the farmer. Then he caught on to what was happening.

Soon Farmer Jake could see over the edges of the steep walls. It was his own kitchen!

"Not again!" moaned Bessie as she looked down into the coffee cup. "You boys always make such a mess."

And what a mess it was! The inflatable tub toy popped out of the big cup of java with Mr. Bunny and Farmer Jake on board, and knocked everything off the table, then knocked over the table itself.

They were home at last!

Epilog

Finally, after the mess was cleaned up, everyone had enjoyed a fresh pot of double-caffeinated cinnamon almond spice mint mocha espresso supreme, then helped poor Ducky Tub Toy when he got stuck in the bathroom. Now it was time for Ducky to go back into Mr. Bunny's magic rucksack until the next adventure.

"Good-bye," said Ducky as he deflated and disappeared into the pack. "Thanks for having me."

"Thank you for being had," said a squeaky falsetto.

"Pardon me?" said Mr. Bunny.

"I didn't say anything," said Farmer Jake.

"Get me out of here!" said the high squeaky voice. The voice came from Farmer Jake's mouth, but old Jake's lips hadn't moved.

"Dang trick tooth is acting up again," explained the embarrassed farmer.

Mr. Bunny peered into Farmer Jake's mouth. He listened with his big bunny ears. Then he reached into his magic rucksack one more time, and pulled out a pair of pliers.

Mr. Bunny hopped up onto Farmer Jake's shoulders and propped his foot on Farmer Jake's jaw and reached into Farmer Jake's mouth with the pliers. He clamped onto something, and tugged with all his might—and out popped a red-nosed molar, looking quite relieved.

"Thanks, Mr. Bunny," said the molar. "I was getting mighty tired of liver-wurst." And out the door he bounced, into the land of cream and sugar we so blithely call the real world.

"He'll make someone a fine mascot," said Farmer Jake.

Mr. Bunny just crinkled his pink little nose and helped himself to a big cup o' carrot juice.

Answers to Exercises

Chapter 2

1. hat
2. ROM
3. into
4. Java

Chapter 3

1. The author had typed 7,000 lines of code before the following solution was brought to his attention.

```
public class SelfList {
 public static void main (String[] args) {
  java.io.PrintStream out = System.out;
out.println("public class SelfList {");
  out.println(" public static void main (String[] args) {");
  out.println("  java.io.PrintStream out = System.out;");
  out.println("  out.println(\"public class SelfList {\");");
  String s =" out.println(\" public static void main (String[]_
args) {\");\n out.println(\"  java.io.PrintStream out = System._
out;\");\n out.println(\"out.println(\\\"public class SelfList_
{\\\");\");\n String s =\"$\";\n for(int i = 0; i < s.length();_
i++)\n   if (s.charAt(i) == 36)\n   for (int j = 0;j < s.length();_
j++) {\n    switch(s.charAt(j)) {\n       case '\\n'_
:out.print(\"\\\\n\"); break;\n      case '\\\"':_
out.print(\"\\\\\\\\\"\");break;\n      case '\\\\':_
out.print(\"\\\\\\\\\"); break;\n       default:out.print(s.charAt_
(j));\n     }\n   }\n   else out.print(s.charAt(i));\n  }\n}\n";
   for(int i = 0; i < s.length(); i++)
    if (s.charAt(i) == 36)
    for (int j = 0;j < s.length(); j++) {
      switch(s.charAt(j)) {
```

```
    case '\n':out.print("\\n"); break;
    case '\"': out.print("\\\"");break;
    case '\\': out.print("\\\\"); break;
    default:out.print(s.charAt(j));
    }
  }
  else out.print(s.charAt(i));
  }
}
```

Of course, the problem with such a self-listing program is that every time the program is changed, it must be changed. Here is another approach:

```
import java.io.*;
public class SelfList {
 public static void main (String[] args) throws IOException  {
    File inputFile = new File("SelfList.java");
    FileReader in = new FileReader(inputFile);
    int c;
    while ((c = in.read()) != -1) {
        System.out.print((char) c);
    }
  }
}
```

Finally, a very efficient self-listing program is shown on page 26. It performs correctly as long as you don't try to run it.

2.

3.It's okay to keep your letter very short and simple. Here's one of mine:

Dear Java-enabled browser,

How are you? I am fine. Aunt Agnes lost her glass eye again. This time it turned up in the spaghetti sauce.

Well, bye for now.

Love,

CE3

Chapter 4

1. A great bunch of guys if you don't mention the nose bone.
2. A walrus with a deadline.
3.

Chapter 5

1. It's not a `while` loop, it's an `if` loop.
2. The statements are separated by Java's *implied goto*.
3.

Chapter 6

1. The variable `i` has not been initialized.
2. Nineveh. (Now don't say Mr. Bunny never taught you anything.)

Chapter 7

1. Squid
2. Squid
3. Squid
4. Squid

Chapter 8

1.

Chapter 10

1. A. Hot Java
   B. Hot Soup
   C. Hot Spring
   D. Cold Oatmeal

2. Geez, you really need a life, don't you?

Chapter 11

1. The method formerly known as "print."

Ask Mr. Bunny

Dear Mr. Bunny: In Chapter 5, you and Farmer Jake were transported aboard a compiler by the tractor beam of a vintage John Deere Model B tractor. However, it is well known that headlamps were never standard equipment on the Model B. How can you explain this discrepancy?
—A trekkie with no life.

Dear A trekkie with no life: I can't.

Dear Mr. Bunny: In the foxhole with Foxy, your rucksack buffer was stomped, apparently by a rogue thread. However, the buffer would not have been instantiated until runtime, and at this point in the story you had not yet even been tokenized. Your credibility is at stake—how do you plan to eliminate such obvious mistakes in future adventures?
—Concerned know-it-all.

Dear Concerned know-it-all: You're hired.

Hey Furball: This is the third time I've posted my question!!! Why haven't you answered???
—Hard to ignore

Dear Mr. Bunny: My dog Bowser is missing. I thought I heard him barking behind the Windows recycle bin. What's going on?
—Timmy

Dear Timmy: Your Bowser is now part of the operating system.

Dear CE3: I'VE HAD ENOUGH! YOU ARE AN IDIOT!
—SORRY, MY CAPS KEY IS STUCK

Carlton Egremont III replies: You seem to have mistaken me for someone who actually exists. Don't feel bad, I've made the same mistake myself. Please direct all future correspondence to the talking rabbit.

Index

List of Figures

About the Author

Carlton Egremont III is a leading authority on himself, having spent many years thinking about this topic to the exclusion of everything else. He has lived a carefree life as heir to the great Egremont grocery separator fortune. As a child he received a nickel every time one of these wonderful inventions was used at the checkout line and to this day each nickel is hand delivered by bonded courier to a gigantic piggy bank in the Egremont back yard, accounting for much of the traffic on the New Jersey Turnpike.

When most children were playing with matches, Carlton played with nuclear waste. He once irradiated one of his father's most important projects, depriving the world of the bowling ball toupee for the next 150,000 years. As usual, punishment was swift at the huge Egremont mansion: He was given cab fare and sent to his room.

A defining moment for the young lad occurred one day on a farm in Wisconsin, when his fate was sealed by the now famous "chicken incident." Carlton had covered the enraged bird with mayonnaise, hoping to make a fresh salad. The Egremonts whisked the traumatized youngster home, where years of therapy failed to reduce his fear of all but the most solidly frozen poultry. But even at a young age it was apparent Carlton was destined to be an idea man.

There were many failures along the way. He developed a dumpster heater (so they can stink in the winter, too), but it never caught on in the tropics. And although the musical toilet paper dispenser was a major breakthrough, a bungled marketing campaign derailed its success as well.

Then in 1997 he wrote *Mr. Bunny's Guide to ActiveX*. He has not appeared in public since, preferring a life of seclusion at the Egremont estate, where a coin-operated doorbell deters most visitors.

Now a Java author, Carlton admits to knowing almost nothing about the language, and insists this makes him the ideal author to write about it. "Other books on the subject are very predictable," he points out. "They have something about Java on every page."

While proud of Carlton's success, the family is of course bitterly disappointed that he could come up with nothing better than a talking rabbit.

The doorbell now requires exact change.

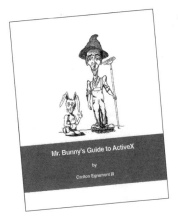

"ActiveX has been around for literally dozens of months, but until now it has remained an inscrutable mystery to all but the most overpaid contract engineers, three Sufi priests, and Don from Nevada. Finally, here is a book that dumbs down the topic so it is understandable even to a piece of shoe leather."

With this single innocuous paragraph, Carlton Egremont III launched the **Mr. Bunny Series** of succinct guides to selected mysteries of computer science.

The **Mr. Bunny Series** is supported, endorsed, and authored solely by Egremont. It is the official place to go when you simply must go someplace official. The books in this series provide no information whatsoever. If you have a problem with that, address your complaints straight to the rabbit, at **http://www.mrbunny.com**.

Egremont was a spoiled trust fund child who has grown up to revolutionize the way we think of…him. He is the author of numerous unpublished shopping lists and is the founder and sole member of the Society for the Advancement of Baby Babble (GWEEP), an organization that seeks to popularize the author's first language.

In 1998, Egremont started all this nonsense by pushing *Mr. Bunny's Guide to ActiveX* at an innocent, unsuspecting public. And in 1999, he forced *Mr. Bunny's Big Cup o' Java*™ down the throats of the stunned programmers who had just finished digesting his first book. No one's sure what acts of intellectual assault and battery he'll launch in the new millennium, but you might try asking those FBI guys who've been tailing him all day.

Mr. Bunny's Guide to ActiveX
ISBN 0-201-48536-2 • 112 pages • Paperback • $14.95

Mr. Bunny's Big Cup o' Java™
ISBN 0-201-61563-0 • 128 pages • Paperback • $14.95